The Snow Poems

By the same author

Ommateum
Expressions of Sea Level
Corsons Inlet
Tape for the Turn of the Year
Northfield Poems
Selected Poems
Uplands
Briefings
Collected Poems: 1951–1971
(*winner of the National Book Award for Poetry, 1973*)
Sphere: The Form of a Motion
(*winner of the 1973–1974 Bollingen Prize in Poetry*)
Diversifications

The Snow Poems

....

A. R. AMMONS

W·W·NORTON & COMPANY · INC·

NEW YORK

I thank the editor of *The Iowa Review* for first
publishing two passages, included here, whose
first lines are, "My father, I hollow for you," and
"when I was young the silk."

Copyright © 1977 by A. R. Ammons. All rights reserved.
Published simultaneously in Canada by George J. McLeod Limited,
Toronto. Printed in the United States of America.

FIRST EDITION

Library of Congress Cataloging in Publication Data
Ammons, A   R   1926–
    The snow poems.
    I. Title.
PS3501.M6S57   811'.5'4   77-4744
ISBN 0 393 04467 X
1 2 3 4 5 6 7 8 9 0

for my country

Contents

Words of Comfort — 1

One Must Recall As One Mourns the Dead — 3

Things Change, the Shit Shifts — 4

My — 6

Here I Sit, Fifty in the — 7

My Father Used to Bring Banana — 12

Have You Seen the Severe Waters — 13

Early October — 14

Terror of — 16

Ivy, a Winding) — 17

The Hieroglyphic Gathered, the Books — 22

Your Full-Service Mover, Madam — 27

When in Early — 30

The Arc — 34

There! The Light of Human Reason! — 37

Hard Lard — 40

Hard Fist — 44

8:45 A.M.—Doorbell Rings: Wife — 48

Shall Will Be Used Properly or Will Shall — 52

No Tirement Like Retirement — 57

Light Falls Shadow and Beam through the Limbo — 61

Mist Curtains Lower and Dissolve — 63

The Snow Is Fine-Sightless Today the Ground — 65

The Hen Pheasants Streak Out of the — 68

Dawn Clear — 71

If You Were Standing under the Elm and — 72

In the Old — 73

Forecast for Today (Winter's Firstday) — 76

I Come In from the Snowy World — 78

Poetry Is the Smallest — 81

Christmas Eve Morning	83
Analysis Mines and Leaves to Heal	86
Snowed Last Night a Lot but Warmed Up	88
Those in Ledge Fright Seek	90
But If the Way Will	92
The Sun Climbs Daily Higher	96
A Seventeen Morning &	97
The First Morning in a Few	102
This Is	104
Quilted Spreads	106
Dung Ball, Round Graveyard	111
I See Downhill a Patch	114
The Stomach Is Quite	117
My Neighbor Shakes Feed along	118
Nature As Waterfalls	119
The Wind Picks Up Slick	122
Cold Didn't Keep the Stuff	124
Teeth Out	128
When I Think of "the Poet	129
You Can't Get It Right	132
The Perfect Journey Is	138
Snow of the	139
The Prescriptive Stalls As	141
After the Dissolve	147
A Sift, Sprinkling, or Veil	149
Structureless Rage, Perhaps	150
Tell What Will Not Tell Direct	152
Spread It Thin	154
Dark Day, Warm and Windy	155
Like Fifty	156
A 41 Morning, Still Cloudy	158
Produce and Fuctifry	162
I Look Up Guff and Find the First	164
One at One with His Desire	167
Dull Lull	171
The Temperature Rose 15 Degrees over	174
As for Fame I've Had It	178
When One Is a Child One Lives	180
Cloud Strays Rounded Up	184
It's Half an Hour Later before	188
This Poem Concerns	190

The Word Cries Out 193
I Woke Up at 6 and It Was 195
A Flock of My Days 197
You Can't Imitate 199
Spring's Old Hat Is Older 202
The Temperature Fell 203
You Can 208
Cunit 211
It's a Wonder the Body 213
Today Was Like Vomiting 215
It's April 1 217
I'm Unwilling 218
The Sky Clabbered Up with 222
A Single Fact 223
It Does Not Rain in 224
One Loves 226
The Miltonic (Miltownic) Isn't 227
My Father Used to Tell of an 229
Arm's Length Renders One 232
I'm the Type 234
Snow Showed a Full Range 237
No Matter 238
It's So Dry the Brook, down 240
Today Will Beat Anything 242
Sight Can Go Quickly, Aerial, Where 244
These Days Most 246
The Cardinal, Slanted Watershed 247
One Desires the Cutting 249
I Wonder If Pagan Is 250
Rage Spells More of My Words Right 252
On This Day Noteworthily Warm 253
Some Nights I Go Out to Piss 254
My Structure Is, Like the 255
You Think of the Sun That It 258
Snow 265
It Snowed All Night Snow 268
Drip Drip 270
Some Fluffy, Long-Swaggly Catkins 273
My Father, I Hollow for You 276
I Knew 277
I Cannot Re-wind the Brook 278

Considering the Variety   280
Variable Cloudiness Windy   282
On Walks I Go a Long Way along   284
One Trains Hard for   286
Will Firinger Be Kissed: Will   288
If Walking through Birdy Trees   290
They Say It Snowed   291

The Snow Poems

Words of Comfort

Words of comfort,
a railing before the fray,
mumbling shock
away from seizure,   between mts
a drone, narrative, longer   wind runs
than mourning, going on over
past the waters of
every expense of care

can modes, syntaxes, rhetorics,
folkways compete
with equanil (I think not)
to put you away) to sleep
(contemporary verse excepted)
(pick up this week's
feelings at your local drugstore)

today misty drizzling (around seventy)
the pleasant pheasant
disappear
drippy-humble
into the shrubs and few
birds bother: crows emphatically find dead
trees to sit in,
skinned branches, line up
into the wind,
a black countercurrent
drippy but cool

get a poem big enough
ocean-sea rivers
stream around it

by the time
a poem is the world

the author is
out of town

pushing fifty—
those years you waited to fill out, you
aren't going to fill out, your
biceps firm up:
past fifty the muscles
string free, lean separations into thew and bone:
pushing fifty, you notice that the
crest due or normal to arrive has
arrived or isn't coming, not
ever coming, not at all, but something else
quite different, that is certainly coming

my friend said
if you can
learn to swim
or fence at
forty or crochet
at forty-two age is just numbers

I go back   odd that
over and often   death the evidence
to repeat myself: for which is
where repetition is absolute
imperfect   is completely
possibility clears incredible

                    each of us
                    exception's single

One Must Recall As One Mourns the Dead

One must recall as one mourns the dead
to mourn the dead and so not mourn too much

thinking how deprived away the dead lie
from the gold and red of our rapt wishes

and not mourn the dead too much who having
broken at the lip the nonesuch

bubble oblivion, the cold grape of ease at
last in whose range no further

ravages afflict the bones, no more
fires flash through the flarings of dreams

do not mourn the dead too much who bear no
knowledge, have no need or fear of pain,

and who never again must see death
come upon what does not wish to die

Things Change, the Shit Shifts

Things change, the shit shifts,
byways and sideways,
break out, horn in,
step in the same do twice

I followed the sawmp
hogs off, I picked meat
with cousinly buzzards,
I got rotten meat out
of the ears of old
raccoons while under
the skin next to the
ground, maggots rippled
in the heat like breezy water

the levelest look's the jaguar's
peccary gaze (deadset to flare)
or the weaving thermal gaze of
the viper for the small mammal, mama
mia, cute frisky little rascal

the curvature of the necessity rides
no more skyward but rounds off,
a comedown comeuppance: in a fallish time,
the birds' gatherings and flights
skim treetops, not
much entering in now, no nests, pausing to consider
or dwell, the wide
storm winter coming

.Envy

Let your friend have
as much of the

world as he can
have, what does
he have: the
wind blows it
away and your friend
also and
you, freeing all
from any trace of taint
*
but because the dust
mills all looks,
tastes, honors fine,
because of that the
small hope
cannot extinguish itself
that some flavor
of the self, indelible
in dust,
qualifies the common end
*
we are abandoned
here to found
our lives on gossamer
distinctions
where steel rusts
& rock cannot hold

My

my
long   slobberer
palaver &   belaborer
palaverer

(biggest old ugliest
awfulest-looking thang)
        Price Slashed (whew)
        For . . .
                QUICK SALE

treetops twittering
birds windily gathering
heading south for
the scallop, scallop-through, in the ridge:
        the jay
        quince-sits
        a minute
        and flies north
into the coloring thicket

when we learn we are trash   I'd rather be
flimsy, flowable, our holding   the flakey
trivial and slight, we must   fool of hope
not say, if that's what   than the
the universe thinks of us, so   smartass
much for the universe: of the
it should be the benefit of our   small and mean
experience here to realize trash
the just groundwork
of marvelous devising, feeling,
touching, tasting, looking,
beauty's unbelievable contrary

Here I Sit, Fifty in the

Here I sit, fifty in the
mid-seventies, the 28th of the 9th, cedarberries
reddening a veil, vine leapage
and leafage red or yellow flame tips in the trees,
the sky mixed
after pure days of rain,
coolishness and windyishness, most
birds gone,
   hi-flo hieroglyphic geese going over,
a day and decade like most any other
if you put in the wind, sun,
believe the brook's fuss,
trees nodding, yessireeing,
the mixture of identifiable hunks of
historicity with permanences and continuos
like geese stringing singings,
the clash and intermingling
within the boundaries of the momentary
and instantaneous of the
perception of the, ah,
all the wavelengths of time, ah, bending in
& out of themselves like coil worms
or worm coils

byways and sideways
forth and back
outsight and inlook

      (in a time of)
      failing powers, physical,
sexual, intellectual, artistic,
belleslettristic, optimistic, etc.,
it's hard (a hair firm)
to keep the slant of the curvature

above horizontal   coelum
without bobbing and dozy dipping
below
into the languorous waters of letting
things take their course & get on by:
no use to wait on you today
nohow, baby, because with the fallings
off of spatiotemporal apples and leaves
and seeds and pods
and skninyings up for winter, in the
and because, ah, of the apple cider and
aster honey and the blue glaze on the
brook slowed distillation-column clear
    and the yellowjackets
    hummed up quiet in the
    stump
    waiting for snow to feather to the door

hard to think of going back into spring,
buds, slender parts, sprigs putting
out, early green and preparation,
then summer filling out, making up,
might as well rush right on through into
ripeness rotten
where like summation or artistic
compression
seeds velvety in the dried-up pulp
summarize recommencement, time's compression

would, some will say, there were
a plain simple thing with a fence round it
    I don't know it seems
possible don't you think plausible a
bit plausible
or perhaps a few
plain simple things with small fences
you say around them
    a cluster or lay-out of them

organized to cardinal points or rated,
axiologically
> rated
> according to

I cut the quince down the other day into so
many stalks it all made a big bundle
upon the lawn high as my head I'd say

but then today I took the pile
thorny limb by branch down to
the limb&branch pile in the bottom yard

I don't care I think for quince, the
thorns, I mean, I am pricked and itchy
here and there including the shanks

some branches got to in the carrying
off well so back and forth which is up
and down (the yard) I went forty times

I think till I began to sweat and stink
and there under the pear tree was a dead
jay, poor thing, which stank in a stream of

whiff which I hit eighty times,
the universal smell of rotten meat not
really an attractive smell when you get

right down to it. . . .

I do not, can not, will not
care for plain simple things
with straightforward fences round them:
I prefer lean, true
integrations of ongoing
with recurrences,
resemblances, half-adventitious or fortuitous

or as some would say accidental,
half-accidental,
not under a third

a live jay lit on the pearlimb (pearl imb)
over the dead jay,
looked down and flicking shrieked & squawked
directly into the dead ear
two minutes (I don't insist
on the meaning, only the facts)
a scolding for dying
or grief trying to make itself heard;
it looked like grief's rage,
a protest like revenge,
grief's blue wings and bright cries!

money can't buy happiness   neither one nor the other
happiness can't buy money   either one or the other
(misery can't buy either)   both (misery loves company)

hark! in my across-and-down-the-street
neighbor's yard, his apple grove all loaded
with red half-rotten apples
smelling good and souring the wind,
a mockingbird singing!
I saw three majestic weeds of ragweed
growing in the ditch and
slipped'em right up out
of the mud and turned their roots onto
the macadam to dry
          this part is called
          the old Intimidation Rag
it is never right to play ragtime fast
it is never right to play ragtime
it is never right to play
it is never right to
it is never right
it is never

it is
it

surface amenities aside
we have little to
go on
except violence and brutality (the long, flat light
of this bright day comes slicing through)

may love   words strip
and least   a man's bones
harm
prevail at
times forever   naked

My Father Used to Bring Banana

My father used to bring banana
stalks home from town
and place them in the chicken coop
so chicken mites would stick
to them
       & a few years ago we had
a flare-up in the local
papers here about feeding layers
crushed oyster shells
to thicken egg shells

forty years ago in Carolina
we used to
bring home a towsack full
of oyster shells every time we went
to the beach

and we had this big old anvil and
big old hammer to
beat up the oyster shells with
       I don't know what became
       of the roosters
       that ate them
       broke out an
       extra set of teeth
my father sure was a mess

this part of my poem is
called chicken (gravy, shit, wing, liver)

sometimes I notice my
shadow and think
there's my father
but I'm fifty now
and it's me

Have You Seen the Severe Waters

Have you seen the severe waters
(how they flow)
have you seen the nodes of high

glass standing or the sharp slants
by the bank where the bank looks for
itself

    I care not what is is   it's up
    what is seems is is   to you
    enough for me

I went to the brook and inquired
what do I have now
how do you mean the bank bushes replied

oh I said
oh I said
and the brook broke saying speak up

so the saying of that day was not
said and the turn that might have been
added to the mind turned away

            clear all day the foliage
            coloring etc the jay loud
            the mockingbird still at it
thickage

Early October

Early October,
fally, papery, yellowy,
watery, raggedy, high
skimmy clouds, brooky
(last week's rains,
now run off, brookly,
cool glass flowing,
metal over slate sweeps)
I'm at fifty Octobery,

not frantic with commencements,
preparations, seedings, searchings
for ways of spring and not
        the rage of
summer, clumpy fulfillingness,
but a throwing of the self out
of gear into gliding's mild astonishment,
letting up into freefall on
rise's other side,
    the leaves still green or
    holding hints hang,
    no longer feeding on light,
    an indifference to purpose,
purpose complete, now
color and high view:

inner purpose given over,
other purposes not one's own start to
clear the stage:

nothing to dwell on, astonishment right
into startled grief,
the rising of settled knowledge that
in a short time all here will

clear and go

why speak of that now,
the pears
hard green after frost's first smart
and the apples
purple-ruddy, burnt onesided:
    still one pauses
    to reflect shallow bemusements,
recall honey,
the inner light of wine,
cold's tang and burn
(good as ever but not as often)

Terror of

terror of
interval
(even with
bridge-note reassurance) the slicing
away into
(dentaljuice) *
depthless discontinuity, whorey bottom
or bottomless horrid,
    too many intervals break up
the road
the sinuous continuous look
out for slides land snow rock
tree blows freshets bridge-outs

neck wires
    hair ties
        sorghum broomcane braided
(vines' rising risks) down
to handles
            log planters
nothing necklaces
cowtooth dangles
                I'm in the swamp I
                must have followed
                the hogs off
awkweird to go to bed with the
chickens and wake up laid

* Betelgeuse

Ivy, a Winding)

Ivy, a winding)
an area, specimen one can keep
coming back to,
a place where, as to school, one can
try out one's explanations
(exegesis is better than no gesis at
all) but
    what
      got me
   about   give
      the   up
      tree
      today
was that
      the leaves
      after a season's
service, their span, serve
fallen: flatten out black
and limber wet and put a film of
chitinous structure on the
ground so nothing
not even a winding vine, can come up and
take nitrogen, carbon dioxide, water, or
room from the tree:
      (they say walnut shells
      falling to the ground
      release an antiplant
      ingredient) imagine!
writing something that never forms a
complete thought, drags you
after it, spills you down, no barrier
describing you or dock lifting you up:
imagine writing something the CIA would
not read, through,

the FBI not record or report,
a mishmash for the fun-loving,
one's fine-fannied friends!
          imagine, a list, a
puzzler, sleeper, a tiresome business,
conglomeration, aggregation, etc.
nobody can make any sense of:
          a long poem, shindig,
fracas, uproar,
high shimmy uncompletable, hence like
paradise, hellish paradise,
not the one paradise where the points
& fringes of
perception sway in and out at once
in the free interlockings of
permanence:
          roots and moles (and grubs) (and
a microorganism that feeds on
carbon monoxide) live in the ground: fish and
ribbonswale and —worms live in the sea:
birds carrying stable mite colonies
and crop-worms live in the air: we, we,
carrying fungal and bacterial residences, our
numberless silent populations, flashy molds,
angry, flashy molds, live, though mainly
in the light, a fine fluid
fragmentation breaks into presence: (any
high consistency, of course,
lacks the differences to know
itself by—hence is unheard, invisible,
unknown, etc) so we are here in a very
great blackness except when the fluid
surfs against a pumpkin, thinning willow,
boulder (any whole thing in space such as
earth) and the disturbance communicates
itself dispersing through molecular
air, a frizzling wide static of sight,
and then the eye's central blackness
none can read or follow creates a

disturbance of color to pick up light
                    disturbances: O
fine fluid, fluency,
and then the
finest highest fluids we've
learned to live in on occasion or for short
visits, the sheeting pulses of the spiritual
                    intelligence which
                    when it breaks
                    against & thru us
                    declares its nature:
   if you would shed light upon a thing
   smash it: or adore it, leave it whole,
              hold to it in darkness:
who will remember us
we cry
yet we will forget
before we are forgotten

if you would explain That Which Is by
structure you would have to locate
the spurs and main beams, sills, joists,
of the put-together, whereas anything
worth taking apart is so put together
it is assimilated
beyond edge, angle, or joint:
niche, cranny, or nookie:
       you can erect skeletons of
structure for their own sake and then
analogize freely: hermeneutic
                    propaedeutic:
good thing June peas
come loose from the continuum:
make a moongate of an
oeil-de-boeuf, make the frangible-invisible
infrangible:

the mind buries to let lie:
times, stations, planes

and overlappings of felt-events give
base and height, structure, to feeling:
vindictiveness, jealousy, greed, alarm,
hostility adjust to deep
dispositions so that reconciliations
and motions at a greater height can be
released as tenderness, concern, delight:
    the error not that the deep
    feelings, found, are heaved up
    but that
    heaving as a form destroys the
    forms of modesty, gentility, and
modulated delight:
    at three I realized
    that my interpersonal relationships
considered for example as a cottonball
of interweavings and
closenesses (a warmth, as of a
mother-centered, father-peripheried
group) were going to be sheared off,
cut through
and that I was going to be a bit of
lint blowing in the irrelevancies of
dissociation: as I grew older
I learned this
more thoroughly:
I write for those who have
no comfort now and will never have any:
I'm delighted that the comfortless are
a minority and
that rosy tales amble otherwise for others:
    I'm not making a fuss:
    I note the determination:
    it is a strict script
written in the injustice of
necessity: I forgive
the injustice, nearly: I no longer cry
to be another, not myself, or seldom:

you who have no comfort
are welcome here, here
with the chaff
alongside the abundant reaping, among
the weeds, after the gleaners:

I am the writing of what was to be but
did not become: your writing
strangled mine:
I make seeing because I have nothing else
& nothing to do in the seen:
bitterness
compels me
to roll my
tongue and spit
a saying
to the loneliness of my unbecoming
unbecoming:
I bring you   no harm that
no harm but   is not nothing
I bring you
nothing

this is "lake country" too: I hadn't thought
of that: indeed, "finger lake country:" see
you top that one (has a small extra finger or

so): course I'm *country* and *western:* I like
music that plinks and means it: *western* New
York: the poetry isn't as good either

The Hieroglyphic Gathered, the Books

The hieroglyphic gathered, the books
numbered and shelved each
to its interior singing, the hum
broken in on or left in high loft
unattended, the quill-conversions to
mock permanence, so many acts
feared, committed or hoped, regretted—
what a relief to go outside away from
the rooms, seminars, policy-committees
to where stability's mode is movement, wind
working with leaves and trash
across the asphalt, windings and
scatterings, starlings flying
into the ivyvine-skein leafless
against the Music building and picking
berries, the clouds fluffy,
pulling apart here and there into blue
sliver-troughs: the freshness
of breaking down, picking,
churning through
versus the artifice
ungathered after all anywhere
except into the fluidities of currency
forever: (that happened yesterday
and only gathered hieroglyphics can
keep it):
     distinguish the long
     arm of the law from
     the member in good standing:
it's pouring rain but I went walking:
the first rain on Dr. Ensworth's dog's
grave, now mounded among the hedge shrubs:
whiff of earthworm

(I almost said earthroom), puddles
fragrant and in the puddles ornaments,
stars of green weed bottom-clear:
from every needletip of spruce
bough, bough on bough, spruce on spruce,
hung a drop-bulb, gray lit:
     will equanil and elavil replace the
trances and spells of religion, philosophy,
art, and madness, theories of depth
psychology or depth theories of the deep:
for, altogether, miltown can do more than
Milton can: luncheon muncheon: more
than fluff and   (l)anguish
less than effluvium: milk is white
blood:

     clouds giving way, the sun broke
out and turned up the voltage
in the bulbs: my fingers are so
cold from the walk (another one) I can
hardly type: chez fuck'n'suck: also no
book like a frigit: and no poem
with a bush you could fly your bird in:
    forecast for today
    were snows and blizzards
    but we may
    have a mere
    high, empty with glory:
        would a collection
        of clarities
        be clearer than a clarity
        or as the collection
        grew would the
        single clarities remain
        clear and
        a great darkness commence
        to surround

or would opposite lobes of clarity
annihilate themselves
into continuum emptiness:

Finger Lakes Painting

I don't like any bush
water won't drip off
except the
two-legged bush, of course, how happy, and
the golden bramble-bush in whose
branches the Sumerian goat's horns, vexed,
tangle:
desert crows,
picky, and the deep desert hawks and
flight-lean eagles, but
walking predators, too, cautious,
big-eyed, and "possessed of a gnawing
hunger to destroy and ingest" as we
artists, so to speak, would create &
dump, only the hunger remaining likewise
stuck in the bush
and mama goat gone and papa off:
leaves fall from the thornbush,
hair and meat from the
goat: skeleton, branch,
the slackened-free entanglement:
the goat thrashes and bleats at midnight
and overhead the desert stars,
big brights (not helping)
and oil underground, the
goat chafing with sharp hooves to
peel and worry down the bush:

       the good of images is
       that they make no
       statement and the bad
       is that they make (evoke)
       numberless statements:

                    (or is that good, too:
                    meanwhile, the statement
                    makes one statement: except
                    in the clump, thicket,
                    or cluster of statements
                    is the image again)
I could write forever, I mean, I could:
I never would
because boundaries, terminations,
determinations give class to held and holding:
        but the imagistes should have
        known that the Golden Calf
        narrows, confines, straitens,
        identifies, and lessens the Spirit
        too much which is shape without
        shape, timeless time,
        visible and never to be seen:
        poems should imitate the spirit's motions from
        the fabulous limitation, so
        golden because so
        striking off temptation, of
        the means, uh:
I can speak big and high
(but to which end?)
I can hone the severe metric,
incision's incendiary:
but honing misses broadcast:
anyway, who would have one around
speaking big and high:
over dishes: filling the vaporizer:
emptying the trash:
prefer chitchat to
swales of the austere unknown:
        neighbor down the street stakes
        his dog out on the lawn, chain
        twenty feet, pretty
        good run: I notice a path of peripheral
        lawnwear, a ring of loss

where the chain, run out, runs
round: the central self unattended,
unworn while the untouchable
other, far and away calls forth
the bark, the slaver, slobber,
scenting: to pull up stakes!
I can talk big: I come
from a land of bigtalkers and
big talkers: what one needs is
the address of relief (relief of
address): (*King Kong* is on—
Thanksgiving classic): summer
for dogs is a conflagration of
smells while winter is the ashes
(snow), a sprig of smoke
rising here and there:
all this poetry
in Thanksgiving on Thanksgiving

Your Full-Service Mover, Madam

Your full-service mover, madam:
your full-service madam, mover:
arouse, attract, specify,
identify, concentrate, propel
and release unmixed, mixed
emotions: I can package
reactions, lob, locate, and lure
centers, keys, knobs,
slots and play upon you as with
or upon an organ:
               go off to a
country, you see things done
different ways: you distinguish fashion
from nature, an educational
distance: but, educated, you're
into fashion more than nature,
a change loosening, shallowing:
               overcast forecast a
true cast but this afternoon is
to open sunny periods, dashed
dashes, clearing exclamation
points, followed by
colonic etceteras:

we need a basis for argument,
argument always we have enough of,
although probably never more
than we need, but though we have
experienced tugging
this way and that
and though we have chipped, honed,
polished, dug and double-dug,
we have failed to find
the single, the first, not to mention

mountain or continent, grain (tiny mew) of
unyielding reality:
   what a pity, many will sigh,
having argued at length over nothing:
but many will be grateful,
locating the necessary recalcitrance
in the unyieldingness to explanation, that
is, finding centers of operations
where, as with juggling, nothing is,
and in contrary motions finding
balance's informed harmony:
explanation explains nothing *away:* get
up the next morning and recalcitrance
has shaded up to opacity again:
think of the medium, the medium's
malleability, explanation works in,
wordy nothingness: then how reassured
we are to risk castles only air and how
delighted to know
that explanation changes just itself,
an arrived-at nothing: whereas,
the work of art (here come the boss)
establishes an empty-centered space,
spiral stabile, wordless where words
may not go,
a recalcitrance of a kind explanation
can only sharpen itself against:

     lukewarm   stand to reason

    the elm I write of is
not the doomed elm, the dutch,
but the siberian,
small-leaved, resistant: the two doomed elms
I had were cut down
and hauled away: just now,
a snowbead shower: the beads fall,
springing, on the greenroofed garage

and roll off the eaves some
but when fall pauses
melt scrubs the white away

(somedays a mist
too fine
to form drops
at the eaves
or shine the highway)
darkens things a
little, though

When in Early

When in early
December everything should be
naked
except spruce, cedar, yew,
here and
there down the side
of a hill or in
a hill's hollow
will be found
a willow's fragile clothes,
yellow dress dropped,
showing the green slip's
shift
of hiding   snow rhymes
       soundwise but
       contrariwise

(being alike in colorwise
one set of   with crow
terms and
unlike in the other
make   oh, my father, you
one whole form said, "someday
overmastering your mouth will
the one polar get you in trouble"
unlikeness)   you were (I've
       made you)
       right
the sheet of and you said,
snow, thin,   "you'll be a preacher,
missing,   like your uncle,"
mingled with loft, close enough, in that
under cedars and I try to give the
such   word life:

under the mailbox   oh, my father,
a wind-mingled   I am one of the few
thinning   left to miss you
                      I do not miss you much

mostly representing the reachable or
available sky
like sky like ground
except for interruptions:
snow's itself's scripture
but in addition
written in it
accumulate actions
reading re-enacts—
the pigeon-toed pheasant,
a hen, I think, walked across the driveway,
short toe inward, long toe, you know,
one foot almost in front of
the other—a mystery and
contemplation, the beautiful, plain hen
color-coded, her signs

our door mouse
houses between the concrete
step and a bottom shingle: every now and
then I catch him streaking for
concrete crack or door crack: yesterday
morning, there was an inch of snow,
(remember)
just enough the mouse could nuzzle under:
he inscribed eventuality on the lawn,
a limber line of snow-collapse showing
behind him: and today, little snow left,
there is the dribble of his feet
over the white blacktop: if it doesn't
warm up more
the paperboy will see

his yesterday-afternoon, snow-pressed,
delivery bike trail

after snow
when evening clears and
night settles
cleared and cold,
crisp forms
on the snow
midforest
and along starry pond margins
and flavors,
scents dry up, lose their stems to sources,
where the dogs
cracking crisp
run:
cold cleanses,
brightens, thins:
if one could save a cubic mile
of this for August!
(magazines advertise
themselves in themselves)

a year, what a year: *anus mirabilis:*
what can you do: the inner ring of
relatives in trouble with
their teeth, fixing, lumbago,
running off in Dusters,
and a wider ring of relatives,
regular mishpucha, coming up for
advice backed up with a loan,
so-and-so's cousin's pill
in the wrong end: what it is:

making baskets

tonight to meet Kammen's guest
Bailyn, the historian, such a nice

man: there were the Novarrs: they
knew Bailyn way back and Ruth calls
him Buddy, imagine, the National
Book Award winner, Buddy, also
the Pulitzer

The Arc

The arc
of
the
loop, the
cradle
of
sway
      to be
      rocked
      in the heights
      (not dropped,
inert, in
earth)

oh, to carry out the byways of
reverie
(the cedars teardrops
before impact)
(something to feel
not just the
discursive unwinding of
feeling)
born we scream
fed we ummm and smack
beboweled we grunt
fucked we groan
and so with death do we tussle and
groan
but why
when in moments of importance
we hold
our tongues
do we give

significance to articulation that
only waits the next
seizure out

      oh, to be rocked in the arm
      of the dwelling, to be
      cuddled and cooed to,
      to whisper and sip, slur
      and loll in the long
      unwindings and squdgings,
      the honey, the honey, oh,
      the honey high,
      oh, the
      air-clear, beer-lit,
      oh, the bright drop,
      retsyn:

eat a pig dinner sometimes and sit
down in a deep chair that rightangles
your uplumping belly out
    cuts off the avenues of circulation
    and boluses of air
    form promoting gastric
    distress:
if it gets severe take a sip
of water, will dislodge
the gasball enough to ease off the
pain but then walk about
to re-establish the circulations
also lift your arms, your hands clasped
behind your head and
let go of your belly or heave out your
chest and meanwhile swing slowly from
side to side this may ease the bubble
up, also it is important to think you
may not be dying, although you will be feeling
like it, because added

tension forms another airball
over itself like those scared, foam-nesting
insects

good reception

fair this morning, much
warmer, over fifty, but
cloudy and rainy in the afternoon
with a falling off of temperature down
to where a few snowflakes flew and
so today was mostly dark and lowering
and blustery but nice

There! The Light of Human Reason!

There! the light of human reason!
issues from the crevasse of that black
hump of hill-line, rounds a
        pastoral fallacy,
is lost behind the Dark Wood,
the thicket treacherous,
but reappears as two, the one
light and its dropped reflection
in the Cavity of Eternal Depth (the
dentist's dream) which is or filled
with water or with a liquorish air of
consistency so that
light will not penetrate it but
throw back up into the world
        but now there goes the progress
        around that awful pit but note
        the light now introduced
into a lantern, flat-sided with panels
in grapy glass, to make it
past
the gash of gorge that strikes
down from the hills through the earth
in a plunge the wind observes
to howl through so that none may pass
unhouseled up (long wait) but there
the faithful light reappears on this our
edge, the long going down into and
arising from, and proceeds onward to
meet us: the light flickers and sometimes cannot
in the whole dark scene be seen but
with tendance and awful looking we may
severally be reminded that reft of this
        bright bit
we sink into greater toothiness and squinting

but so much for the story if
no end to the story's glory (glory's story?)

                                    what is
matter's project here, is it, where every
hub is afire with spinning and every
axle taking on the resonance of a
dissonance, where every next instant has
a twelve-ton meteorite or thousand-foot
ledge-drop in it, where everything
one once loved drains backward away into
a common hole, where underfoot one
feels time's shimmy, the sludge- and
sledgeweight of gravity's maw,
where nothing that in this fair
day takes on brilliant delimitations
and delights will miss tomorrow's
indifferent spill, waste, or fill or gravid
mud

(I can hardly care a paragraph for such
fidgeting)
              (when the downswoop collects us
will we look into the sky's
mild mien or
back on an
earth we haven't learned to lose)
              matter
projects
the breeding of races crusty, to fall
asleep in calamity's bosom, power
too self-effacing to bear its own
strength, that can be the patient nurse . . .

The X Press
The X Press Press
The ReXPress

bound and determined
metes and bounds   sky-high
ground meats   meets

Mr. Spilldiddler
Mr. Dillspiddler
                    rough day
                    stuff tough

Hard Lard

Hard lard hard fact
hard wind hard core
hard ball hard time
hard hard

the clouds lower low dipping almost
skirting skinny-brittle treetops
but drop a ground-brightening!

the snow, pleasant flakes, dry
enough to worm in the wind
before touching down
or brushing stopped against bush, brush,
garagedoor handle or what, even the
clothesline a skinny, longwinded catcher:
people are good for you if nothing
much ails you but if people (cruel
and insensitive, survival pluses) ail
you nature is a rescue, go to it,
nonpersonal, decommissioned, an
indifference big enough to cool off or
melt down
your differences: sometimes,
when it seems the mind will hesitate,
swell in a realization and break,
and one thinks that perhaps one may
fall down or wobble past resilience,
then one turns with relief to nature,
the verbal empire's blocks, pigeonholes,
axioms, pronunciamentos, and stuff (stuffiness)
chewed up in the simplest
wind-sand design or snow flurry: oh, to
break through the strangling entanglements,
binds, clusters of wordy mentality and
feel the luster of woodsfloor under snow!

vitiated by arrogance, jubersome
of seriousness, my language
will hardly touch stumps or stump: if words
hurt me, why do I
come to them to move a saying through:
am I saying in words how I wish nature
in fact were, though impersonal: fluent,
yielding, showy, a dance of mind not
words (though in words) but things:
I could get something straight but
it would stop winding:

with words to make nature sound off,
speak up
till we find the place where it
will say nothing further,
be of no further use, an example to
no further imposition,
an illustration of, allegory of, nothing

so that we can achieve the podium of
inhumanity, the clearing, wherefrom
we can look back and away to the
astonishing thing, man's rise and demise,
and then what, the crazy universe here,
here, here for thousands, even millions
of years, going on with purposes, if
any, not ours: room
enough for every correction of view,
where perspective is never sold out, utero,
utero, the
commencement before the commencement:

snow sounds like gritty pellets
on the panes:
I thought it was a mouse in my paperbox:

here's a little poem I jotted down this
morning: it's about a complete action,

ah, except for the purple do: the starlings,
having hung sideways on the music building's
ivyvine collection while picking the berries,
sit meditatively high in the branches of the
oak to rest and then the berries
that had not fallen from the vines fall
from the lofts of oak, empurpling do's
sparse rain:

       the starlings barely
       got the berries
       off the vines

       before snow
       lineations loaded
       them up again

once there was a maple tree: during
the summer it produced lots of
maple seed: when the leaves fell,
clusters and clusters of dry maple seed
were left, ruffles, hanging in the tree:
when the first snows came, squirrels
were often in the maple tree eating seeds
and, soon, most of the branches were
empty: one day a dog came by and startled
a squirrel as he was eating from a cluster
of seed far out on a branch: the squirrel,
leaving one seed in the cluster, stopped
eating and ran back to the trunk to go
up higher in the tree: but the dog went
on and the squirrel turned back to eating:
but not back to the single seed
far out on the branch: hard cold set in
one day and for weeks no squirrels came
out: then on a warm windy day in March,
two maple seeds, the only two left on the
tree, softened in their stems and blew

away: one seed fell on the macadam and
the tires of a car crushed it: the other
seed, the one the squirrel, interrupted
by the dog, had left behind, fell next to
the garage between two rosebushes: that
was the sunny side of the garage, and the
rosestocks helped hold the warmth, so the
seed germinated and soon was a tiny tree
with a leaf of its own: I thought, my
goodness, all the maple tree's seeds
produced one tree, but I
couldn't have a tree that close to
the garage so I pulled it up

a poem is a machine made out of worlds
a poem is made of words fed to machines

hard fart   hard tack   I feel so much
hard ware   hard sell   better on my
hard head   hard boil   feet provided
                            I have something
                            to lean against

Hard Fist

Hard fist
hard turd
cool whip
soup dip
freezer queen
candy 6pack
full quart
good thru
strawberry preserves
boneless ham
personal butcher
save more
windshield washer
raisin bran

will all
my talk
not dissolve
reticence's pellet,
dishonorable silence's
unwanted bead

rarely has so much
been said over so
little unsaid

big wig

pay attention
pay no mind

"up yr nose
with a rubber hose"

"up your dick
with a toothpick"

in yr ear
with a hornet's rear

"up yr ass
with a blade of grass"

many fears are born of
fatigue & loneliness

scraps from, the trash of, the verbal
environment
saved, retention's waste, waste's
retention, the scary, sublime,
heavy musk anal honey, but also
the collection, munitions
    for colonic assault

save a life
return my dog
my brown and white
female dog was taken   Record
from the Straight
Lobby Friday Dec 5   My wife, the
she is my closest   weightlifter,
companion and I am   smiles and three
destroyed without her   tons
    (from a bulletin board)   rise from my back

Go   lemon juice
            crabmeat claws
Old age   swiss slices
gets   salad shrimp
set   lean roast
to sit   baking mix
down   apple sauce
            pie filling
            ground chuck
            minced clams
            corned beef

the elm
also (like the   in
willow) late   this
to lose   our
its leaves   own
has (like   day

the willow)   and
lost them   time

arrange these words so that they make
sense
                              people, self-centered,
inconsiderate,
cheer news of a darkness darker
than theirs, a deeper gouge
into a wound more rotten:
least can they bear news
of a happiness close to them

I side
a minority of myself
with the majority
against the majority
of myself
which is a minority

there it is
equation-tranquil
mesh it   make little
with life and   of much
it can (almost   make much
unfailingly will)   of little
break   or
down   make little or much
or short circuit   of much
                       and little

I won't weep
though:
the rhetoric
"make a big fuss over nothing"
is not a good poetic,
not even a
good idea,

not even
"make a big fuss over something"

make molehills
of mountains

8:45 A.M.—Doorbell Rings: Wife

8:45 A.M.—doorbell rings: wife
answers: voice says, "Good morning,
I have a chest for you."

wife says, "Right up the stairs."
I'm right up the stairs on the stool,
door and butt cracked; here they come:

conceptualization is
self-correcting (don't worry)
and not as bad as I've made out, I've
made out: for example, imaginative
forms derive from bioforms, take the
maindrifts and subtleties: the big
channel moves away from the heart of
the matter directly and sizably (as
to volume) but then, moved away, begins
to correct itself
to the pressure
to break down, lessening in—
to distinction so as
to become available
to organs, tissues, and cells,
to establish deep and wide application
    and relevance: but there rationality,
        though at its sharpest ramification and closest
to its immediacy, commences
to break down, the mind unable
to bear so much division of matter
    with no lessening of rationality as
        "form:" the mind reacts with dullness
to
too much subtlety and falls asleep:
    but just as rationality has lost its way in—

to contact with every body cell, there it
    corrects itself, having achieved an
    ocean presence, where distinctions are
    so slight and multiple, they assume
    the wide look of universal constitution:
    the mind, refreshed by that playing
    out, at least, returns slowly
    through the capillaries, regathers
    itself in—
to its main drifts and
    considerable matters and, announcing
    itself, returns
to the circulations:
I think I already wrote about (or
thought about) this but
the alimentary canal as river with falls, lakes,
etc. is a good form, also the form
expansion-contraction: lot
of them, probably, all finding
ways to play in the imagination,
too: how delightful:

I saw through the earth once:
a clearing-through as if of light:
terror made the light, drilled it through:
the earth spindled, insubstantial as life:
another fellow saw through, once:
I hope the shakes did not shake him long

kill time

expect turmoil, gusts, shifts in stone,
expect the arms of change to spin
but allow the Singing Sage
to slip by on his Big Boat singing
        Turmoil is Illusion
        at the Heart of
        the Great Peace

bedrock nestles
in flow
and flow rides
highways
tips of flame plume:
but under that,
deeply within,
the most fluent fluid, motion,
establishes the citadel

I can see but little,
and that with much leaning,
of the elm from this window and
indeed no part of that attached to the
ground but outbuoyed branches only,
mostly tips
nevertheless
possessing curvature of definition
in the uttermost, the tips ending in an
invisibly inscribed continuity or
configuration of nothingness:
    if I worked in the other room
    next to the elm
    (a winter-sunny room)
    I'd get to know more about
    the elm
    but so much more would dominate
    the poem: to want a poem about
    an elm is not to want a poem
    too much so, or too much poem
    too much so: if I need more
    elm to say, I can
    mosey over and peer
    out into further information)

overwhelm whelm helm elm

        this day bluedog clear
        I stood in it absolutely

<pre>
               unoccupied a minute and
               said how sharp the world
               that cares nothing for
               us is
               but now at dusk,
               billows come up
               over the west looking
               solider than hills
               and black and blue with
               snow, I think
               how is it possible the world
       so entertaining and extravagant
       has nothing to do with us (on a personal
       basis) though we
       in the formation of gene arcs, contours,
       sweeps, saliences, and spirals
       were tested bit to bit by
       billows, swell of snowwind,
       bright our sandy river,
       and found to survive the astonishments,
       coping, throwing them back:

          behind bars

       when I have studied the elm
       I hope to devote myself to the weather,
       majors and minors of substance, the high
       substance nothing is done about, the
       low showers narrowed into washouts,
       the happy variabilities day to day
       winding round the deep variabilities of
       season (reason, treason): the year
       cycles, sunspot cycles,
       micro, meso, macro: bi:

       it's too dark to see to write:
       gather it up and rip it off
</pre>

Shall Will Be Used Properly or Will Shall

Shall will be used properly or will shall
   here near
   midDecember
   grayworks (if we have
   hit the deep a falling off
   dismal,   we'll fall
   days clipped into a
   off on   falling out)
both ends till you can
hardly find the middle
but then comes a winter
festival (festival
estival) inaugurating
longer light

   the city that cares
   for tares   (egad,
   has no need gasso,
   for weeds   glorybe)

the M Sea bore
Civ, unhappy
daughter
(dumping the dump from 400
million sets of human guts
plus industrial scours, washes,
rinses) now killing
the mother,
a daughter who unless made a Bridegroom
of Intelligence
must swoon away into
self-poisoning unredemptive guilt,
  whereas

with Wisdom for the weed,
Care for the ground cricket
(whatever is good for the ground cricket is
good for the country)
Concern for the undersea
rocky ledges of octopuses
the mother might
still have lineations of
life left which, clearness drawn deeply into,
would begin to show again
an image Mother Mediterranean:
                    but nothing is to be
                    expected of man, his
                    intentions tedious &
                    mean: by accident
                    he is wise or noble:
                    he sees not his life
                    one life among many
                    kinds of life, every
                    kind attuned to a
                    careful impulse
                    that lets it boom
                    and loll in its own
                    dwelling: Civ,
inconsiderate daughter, maker of weeping,
unnaturalizer, fabricator of
fabrications, pretender to feeling, huzzy,
it would hardly be unfair if
Sea gobbled you up so you could not harm
Forest, Icecap, Deep Trench, or Friendly
Breeze again, baby:

natural gas is okay on a cold night and
antibiotics are so fine when you need them:
but man's fabrications aren't as subtle
and resilient, flexible, accommodating
as natural complexes: why can't we proceed
but show the proper respect:

FreshLARGEEggs
This carton is bio-degradable
a contribution to environment

(also, what are we to do with it if
you bring it back) a contribution, tribute,
offering, tithe
as if to the new god: ok then a few more
worshippers will do it:
              playacting:
              playoffs:
              (Redskins, Raiders, Steelers,
              Colts, Dolphins, Cowboys)
              (look, cavity, no moms)
              poeticules shrink up
              into starved strategies
              and strive to prove
              skinny devices significant,
              but I, I mean . . .
nothing works without a nearly
equal tug the other way:
and then one is fifty and feels oneself
(if no one else will) (no one else will)
in the tug of
a tendency, as if one were an
impurity rushed through
various waters
to the kidney of selection
where the organism engages in certain
abandon:
but the mind, imagination, is only getting
fresh at last, wind free, ready for
treetop castle or diamond waterfall,
recalcitrance flowing loose, a clear honey
to the embrasures of sight:
truth's a show,
a good one one that does not end before
the audience leaves: that holds

up a cranesweep of meaning,
snakes or eels or noodles, great
wound-up unwindings, heavy, light: that
lets no direction or effect grow pure
without contrariwisdom, counter-purity:
    say not what
    I have made
    say what made
    I have cut
    free of:
Sumerian, Egyptian, Greek, Roman,
European, Holy-Roman, Anglican: we have
hills old-low,
    lines of windbreaking lombardies:
    windrows:
    thickets wind-settling:
    spruce nook moving nothing, resident
authorities

	big rig
spoontang	big zig
spoontongue	big cig
dongtong	big fig
dungtongue	big MIG
tightassed tightend:	big dig
eternal journal:	big pig
	big gig
	big jig

mindgoggling:
    the poet abandons a
    place to the reader

I sometimes catch myself
fearful I've
let out the news of death,
told more than people will
please to hear,
a news, though, nowhere to be
kept still:

it flies loose and about
and is (must be) told in
every ear till
told too loud
no one's there to hear

ass/mind balls/heart
ball loose flag down

it's 4:20 dusk coming
the Redskins have a touchdown
to go with their fieldgoal

Phyllis made seven fruitcakes
undetermined square or round

No Tirement Like Retirement

No tirement like retirement
no floppage like stoppage
busy busy boys and girls
old geezers,
strungout ninnies (no
                    treads
                    like   threads
                    retreads)
having made avocation vocation
I must now
rise through
making vocation avocation
so I can spend
    my
time rusting   (l)agony

dressed, undressed, redressed

use is the best polish
(drooping thru the chills of the
                              sorghum to
where the spinnet's broke)

    after so many days of
    mingling, cloud and hill,
    mists, skirts of vapor
    dripping and valley-dragging, fringes,
    brushing ghosts
    through hillbrush, moon
    and soon
    I mean sun
    clorox twins

everything lifted this morning and there

between the devil and the deep blue
between a rock and a hard place
between a cliff and a sharp slope
was the source bright,
                    looking central

a warmish morning walkable and how musty
I'd grown far off from the lean, mean
brook
its quick scars of light
its breaking, regathering,
ledges and clear heights underwater,
its mosslawned banks, rock terraces,
tangled vestment vine
      (choked trees
        deadwood trellises)
                (those with
                inclinations to
                sprawl on
                you, spurn,
                sprawl on them)
if you come into the world
with an unspeakable structure or
stricture to speak,
a weird move to the freak fringe,
then you got an insoluble
problem, an
"immedicable woe"
you got a sore with a lifetime supply
of scabs, you is, in other words, in
business
      the average person is average
      the common people is common
      the straight people is straight
      you gone be the crooked weird
      rare intelligent bird creep type
      that what you gone be, honey
                you gone look funny

when they put you in your
coffin
like you something
unright
like you ain't
worth dying
like every day when they passes out the
honey
you gone get a little vial of fear and
you gone drink it yes you is
cause tomorrow when they passes out
the honey again
you gone git another one of those little vials
and what you gone do with them vials
honey better go head drink up one at a
time
cause you gone have something to
shake about too
while the others is shaking with
the sweetness
you gone be breaking out in the high
jives of terror
shaking like you done met up with some'm:
I hope no young'un mine
go through with that
(salt talk with a dash of pepper)

being there is the next best
thing to long distance

may I by
being me be
you for you

                    trust money
or will you   and trust people
take my I   to try to get it
to be you   away from you

for a minute
as I will
take you

                               looks like an
                               all-day gray

to be I
when I can
maybe your you

Light Falls Shadow and Beam through the Limbo

Light falls shadow and beam through the limbo
limbboughs, short and long mixtures,
lineations,
staff and heading, balling the
boughs, clusters, white bass clefs
churning rotund
thunder and up there sparkling and
bellying out
skeins and scads of treble felicities,
cones and points:
tree as music in the light,
the scoring of the permanent
enchantment,
a presence not regular but hastening
or not like the imagination or
the wind
and telling

nothing but that though the gorge roars
and though
sodden swatches of forest spill
from a high ravine and though
a beaver is shut in by a boulder time
will slowly budge
and though we ourselves see and do not
know what we see and cannot tell why
we are here attracted to enchantment
and scriptures intermingling substance
and light—
        oh, the hillways, passes, the peaks
        of the thoroughly achieved!
some such dwelling in the light,
hardness in the ray,
the interpenetration

that in leaving, separating out,
never leaves out,
that bringing things still again runs away
also with everything into night

Mist Curtains Lower and Dissolve

Mist curtains lower and dissolve
the ridges halfway down
(imagine
a thunderstorm predicted
for midDecember,
55 but
no thunder yet: rain,
though)
      1:01
      1:00
        :59   downspouts

   the threequarter
   moon at midnight
   shining from a
   high sky's well
   on this host of
   hills, the lake
   off to the side
   there glimmering
   in a big space,
   a Christmas tree
   crystalline with
   colored lights
   down a near slope,
   way over the valley
   a string
   of glitter, a
   highway, ropes a
   slope: how can we
   be here: how is
   it possible, here
   with earth moon sun
   these people these

myths and dreams:
were we not here
we could never
be
thought of:

> oxbows of
> highway rise
> like a
> small elation
> over the opposite
> ridge

The Snow Is Fine-Sightless Today the Ground

The snow is fine-sightless today the ground
brightens white for no cause
and the green garageroof
is all at once side-white

    the elm's grooves and streaks
    of bark are highlighting: it's 28
    again to be 10 tonight

                make
all the fuse that's lit to glint   a
one handy tool (ah)   difference

arm milk   when we
eye cunt cheese have nothing
hip shit   significant
leg come   to say
ear blood   spelling it
toe wax   right matters
lip eye cracklings   (makes a
jaw snot   difference)
rib spit

I reckon
cornholers get dooky
on their tools (and yucky blood)
time's dust is a rinse
nothing resists

to get the spook off language,
the microphone, pulpit, lectern, the high
whines and
    broad moans out,
    scald and rinse every word

till it takes on and gives off
the exact hue (drift)
for for
the most part
language moves our lips while
we grind, hiss, haw—
let the words have no rich soup
they cannot themselves generate

if fellows burr, hum, buzz, loop
break out strict shears
snip ropes from the heavy molasses to
hang those fellows with

tipping from pole to pole
we flash through uprightness, stability,
truth but
    unchanging reality
    is the polar extreme's
    intolerable
    exaggerated weather

the temperate zone the land of soft announcement

one desires leisure, ease, if
those are to be desired, when one
might desire action, stress, doing
as being, too, ideal

I write this to be writing,
wife gone off with a stationwagonload
of women to Rochester in the snow,
son at school,
    office hours this afternoon,
    meeting,
    Christmas coming,
    me home

go through

I'm not sure there's enough light
out there to make a day of
                but look
a patch of blue the size of a man's hat:
it could grow into a radiant clearing,
blue inanition, dome of
high feeling, starvation

when a father dies
the sky comes unlooped from the stars

The Hen Pheasants Streak Out of the

The hen pheasants streak out of the
thicket
down the hedgeline through the
yard

selfcentered shortsightedness

    fag pag jag
    feg peg jeg   trouble
    fig pig jig   shovel
    fog pog jog
    fug pug jug   stir-fry

is life a	is life a	a puzzlement
show death	show truth	a bit of
corrects	kills	a difficulty
or is	or is	
death a	truth a	
show life	show life	
corrects	kills	

as you go into life (some say they
wish they were alive or dead) you must
forget where you're going
which is into death
but as you go into death you must begin
to take a more general and perhaps
generous view of life, and not be
so particular
but that may be the difficulty
that we are heavy
to relinquish our made selves,
mirrorments, to the trust of the

great unwieldy, unspecific self:
in these transmissions
we are not like to be consulted:
our talents turn to attitude:
verbal flak:
  (a bishop or royal personage
  displays his
  flabella, a touch to the
  human that he sweats)
picking up brilliants, bowerbirdwise,
etc., or as with the builder
of beercan palaces, tidbits, also, of
tile, mirror, sherd, whatever with a
paste, mortar, of cogitation, sealing
throughout making of-a-piece: but if
you seek brilliants it's
no matter what shines:
the value is apparent in apparent shining
  but those who dwell upon
  and on the invisible
  value not the visible
  apparency
  not diamond-shine
  but rarity or hardness
  so invisible

to deal with muddlement
which is not
just a mixture but
a single speaking of multiple clarities
(very puzzling unless the
clarities are so small
as with sand
they will lose their special identities
to a general view)
to deal with muddling or muddlement
confine the currency of inquiry
within fairly narrow banks urging

and also guiding flow
so that means can go out among the
areas and question closely
so to speak
or drop bits of matter at the roots
of things so that answers may grow
(we need have faith
only
that of course currency is
winding
that can never wind away,
cannot go far without returning,
an observation
so succinct
faith
is perhaps too high a shelf to bother)
when I look death
in the eye
my pavilions quiver
and my crystal battlements
and walls of high castle
dance in the afternoon breeze

    this one
    death swept
    shape

    broken off from the
    earth broken off
    from the mother

    spent now except
    for the flicker of
    burning out

supposed to get cold tonight
the ephemeral lasts because
it's back fast

Dawn Clear

Dawn clear
by sunrise
hazes riffles   you want to be
furrows and floats   bullfucked when
of fluff   mine is no longer
appear   than a penguin
so the sun
has too much   quilt raffle
to come through   antiques
to come through   handcrafted gifts
                       live country music
make verbal   whimsies, furbelows, and
things tangles   sundries
mazes puzzles
clusters   bitter winds
consonances   clink the tinkle
dangles knots &   bell in the tree
stuff to have   and find
something   cold's exact key:
to fool with   the big male
when time has   pheasant sulls
a bigger presence,   low on one foot
margin, than
things or actions
I make things
and abandon
them for you

the sun didn't do much for us today
but it de-snowed the garage roof
and left a crop of
smallish icicles down the eaves-row

If You Were Standing under the Elm and

If you were standing under the elm and
looked up it would be dark
but if you were above it (flying?)
and looked down it would be
white:
    dust or flurry snow, the fine
sifty stuff, has not missed a twig,
hiding it from the sky: but if it
gets windy and wrenching or if a
crow lights somewhere and flaps his
wings squawking, then
darkness may be noticeable

In the Old

In the old
days
of vaginal, or coincidental,
sprays
    hairpie diners
    could have plum
    tart, peach or
    strawberry
tart (in the old days words didn't buy
much)
    get more   pedazo
    out of   de
    going out   burro

authentic theatrical
forms with
mimes, masks,
    puppets, processionals, players
        (singers
keep   groups
my   bands
word   writers
     composers)

    islets and islettes
informal (isles)   formal (tisles)
      soup aisle
    aisle de soup
    do-ahead dough

super bargains in vinyl flooring
roll-ends for bathrooms, entryways,
      pantries, laundry rooms
grind

she said this afternoon that
because of the snowsqualls she
might have to put a damper
on her shopping expeditions

the sun came out enough
to moon
behind the snowclouds
    so, everything loaded,
      there'll be no unloading
today
unless by dusk the wind comes unsprung:
the hemlocks,
sculpture all day, now
nod in the breezy free-ends
     ohyesohyes

     so many whales plundering through,
     more whaleback than water

hemlocks made to order
to hold snow
were also made
limber to sway snow
loose
or at least hang unsplinteringly
in white
holding:

     lamb sandwich

Namath, ribs bruised, limped off the cold
field today, Shea Stadium snowy, windy,
four days before Christmas, Namath who
broke all showing-them-how's expectations!

if we are reluctant   if only one could
to step into the field   make or find a bit of

when it is our time
we may be reluctant to leave
the surroundings
when our time
has passed

wisdom that turned
through a situation
or two would hold
still or still hold

it's after sunset
cloudy
cold and gray
but tomorrow is
to reach the mid-thirties

Forecast for Today (Winter's Firstday)

Forecast for today (Winter's Firstday)
(you may
recall) was
thirty-five or so (which hasn't seen
twenty yet)
beefed up this morning by a promise of
sunny spells
but now at five minutes to one the drifty
tinkle of snowflakes
merely continuos: a few minutes ago,
in truth,
a blue patch appeared sky-high but the sun,
wintering elsewhere, wasn't there so
nothing hit the ground here:
couple three months ago
I cut a grapevine out of the big cedar
to reduce weight's becluttering darkness
but here the snow's
getting into the tree as much as
grape leaves shaded light out:
    at dusk a flock of pheasant
will be-wing, shrieking rusty flanges, up
and beheist themselves,
belaboring beswung boughs:
        the squirrels in the thicket
        had such a good time this fall
        up-and-down winding
        chasing each other
        I bet there isn't a flake
        of loose bark unfallen
        on a trunk
        in the whole blame thicket

        all I ever know is
        rigor between the shoulderblades,

lumber in the gut,
hard theory-light in the head:
I process life by shaking,
I'm a sifter: I wish I were limber
and relaxed, able to affirm the self
and take from the world a small taking

limberer than lumber

I swerve attention out of the mix of
myself into the outerness where otherness
can conjoin my outerness whereas
only I can look into myself
and I spend enough time doing that

the sun broke out before setting
but set behind new clouds moving
in: the Christmas tree's up and
John & I have bought presents,
everybody has bought everybody presents

I Come In from the Snowy World

I come in from the snowy world
of muffled roads and she says
how's the outside world
and I say
still outside (gotterdattoom)

Giants Beat Saints

you can't step forward with
both feet on the ground

proverbs suck up recalcitrant reality
and spit out a beam of light but
emerge among them
systems of conflict, divergence,
contradiction: too many
proverbs obstruct the view
but enhance the reality:
not the wisdom but saying's finding:
   the middle regions
toilet paper chinks cracks
against excessive windiness:

               jocundity

the beswirling elm this morning was attacked
by white bees

last night after sunset the weather
warmed up, night-snow-blue clouds
heaped on the horizon,
holding, glowing underneath in earthshine
   in winter here
   the sun arcs a

southern circle of small compass
and has
slight surface relation
to temperature
except
ice will melt off a car or
highway great
in direct radiation
but it warmed up last night after sunset
to twenty-five and the fronds and
jungle foliages (that make
in teens climates)
ran off the windows, thaw's
deconstruction:
how does a running back hold it

                sight
                feeds on a
                medium
                whose
                source blinds
                but no big
                sound gives
                off little
                earfuls
although the ear can be exploded
   (not death
   but life can   one forgets
   be   before one
   missed)   is forgotten

   the squall   a bit of
   comes on   dried hydrangea
   from the west blossom
   across the lake comes loose and
   with the sun the wind
   behind it   rolls it
   suffusing it, over a yard of

oblivion melting   snowcrust the wind
everything   variable
                   enough to
                   play
                   the blossom with us,
                   no, there it
                   goes behind
                   the garage

on the way down
but then the
squall hits
with fierce soft
mingling

snow
ghosts stand up
and walk off the roof

Poetry Is the Smallest

Poetry is the smallest
trickle trinket
bauble burst
   the lightest   f
windseed leaftip   r
snowdown   e
poetry is the breaks   e
the least loop   d
from   o
    the general curvature   m
into delight
poetry is
the slightest   f
hue, hint, hurt   r
   its dance too light   e
not to be the wind's: e
yet nothing   d
becomes itself   o
without the overspill   m
of this small abundance

you don't mind, do you, I
said to the mountain, if
I use this ledge or, like,
inspiration pavilion to say

a few things out over the
various woods, streams, and
so on: by all means, said
the mountain: I was a little

concerned, I said, because
the speech is, like, about   only
the individual vs the major   where

structures and, like, I

was thinking of siding with
the individual: but, of
course, said the mountain:
well, but, I said, it

doesn't make any difference
what I say if it doesn't
make any difference: please,
said the mountain, be my guest

a slice of clearing
widened over the ridge at
sundown and the sun
stood in it a minute,
full glow flapping up against
the garage and trees
and through the windows against
the walls and it was very nice
say around four twenty,
gold effluvia gone
by four twentyseven

poet friend of mine's
dick's so short
he can't pull it long enough
to pee straight with:
not to pee on
anybody by surprise
sideways, he hunkers
into the urinal so far
he looks like, to achieve,
relief:

we
are
to
lose
all
are
we
to
have
here
and
there
a
trifle
only
where
we
are
to
lose
all
are
we
to
be
here
beholding
everything

still his fat wife's
radiant every morning:
he humps well, probably,
stringing her out far and
loose on the frail hook:
and, too, I notice she
follows his words
closely like one who
knows what a tongue can do

Christmas Eve Morning

Christmas Eve morning
a sifting of snow
blurry clouds
with near-clear spans of western blue
still at nine
nothing coming through in beam from
the east
    the hemlocks rocked and
    winded yesterday
hold their old darkness back today

to have fun you have to need it
so little you don't need any

you fear the grave   if you won't
so much it is   change yourself change
possible before life is   the world
done with you you
will beg for it   change the world you
    won't change yourself
this year's been
so horrible even the
thought
of improving it
is frightening

then the sifting thins into a sheen of
micro-lights, pane crystal flints,
twinkling down like fog-fuzzy bugs through
beams of early sun,
derived not from clouds but a haze
that barely pales the sky

weather is continuo to the clustral or choral

the deep through-going that adds a middle
to islands, glaciers, ponds, fields, woods,
to rain, or snow, or wind or
   the sun's weather is
   continuo
   to earth and Mars and
   elsewhere
or the galaxy's (here we go again) shine is
continuo
within which gather and move chords,
concerts, aggregates, configurations,
tangles, thickets
which in turn turning feed into and move the
                         continuo:
clapper-hung bulls tinkling bells
balls on icy highweed

          spot of marsh there
          in the meadow
          cattails and redwings
          artesian source
          a bog going
          around saved

the tree-mingling mists
on the high gap's ridge
seem not a nature
my self, too, inhabits, brushing up
against the rockface,
leaking from boughs
   but another dimension, intention, or
working that asks neither my
compliance nor participation

buried yesterday afternoon
today Uncle Emory
begins his first
full day in

the grave, the
whole round of
the dark service,
the wageless hours
and hourless wages

but what a brilliant
finish to the snowstorm
(another due tonight)
so much sun I sat with the jade
plant half an hour
while sheaves of brightness
fell across its deep leaves
and, eighteen the high, here and
there direct light caused icicles
to form out of hung snow,
the ridge on my
metal mailbox turned into a single
long icicle, dog's tail

Analysis Mines and Leaves to Heal

Analysis mines and leaves to heal
clouds, coasts along the way but comes
to recourse's nothingness to heal itself

during the night
the wind pulled
up a cloud cover
patchworks
aprons   my wife says
hotpads   you can't learn
place mats   magic by magic
skirts
lunch bags

intercourse is better than no course at all

hardly able to take a frail wind
or thin change in altitude or
attitude, we measure riffles,
waves, ounces, vibes for power,
scrupulous tissue

axioms, postulates, theorems, hypotheses,
hypotenuses, conclusions, paradigms in
neat blue conic sections, curved lines, dots,
lines, and planes, cubes, prisms, cylinders,
spheres, all that good stuff

temperature goes up, snow falls:
break out the stars,
cold shines them: stir up a southern breeze,
here come the windchillindex

here, indeed, we're eating dead chicken (stuffed with

stuffing) cranberry sauce, applesauce,
white potatoes, broccoli, salad with
dressing including one dark olive, cookies
and ice (dark olive how I luf you) cream
and cake and the snow outside coming down

Snowed Last Night a Lot but Warmed Up

Snowed last night a lot but warmed up:
today has been cloudy
unsnowing and up to 40 maybe 45:
icicles have dived off eaves:
the hemlocks
which keep fine clumps
are unsnowed
tipsy with breeze

I got a plant collection
for Christmas, jars, cups, liqueur & other glasses,
potted and planted,
but I'm doing tiny plants
I like my loyalty
and their precariousness

                              the big round yew
                              has five thick floes
indoor green   of snow on top
                              too central
                              to angle off, fall
                              away
the maple's fleshy underlimbs look spooky,
more light bounding up from the
snow than falling from the gray near-dusk:
        I shoveled
        wet-bottomed snow out to
        the garage, where I got the peat moss,
        then out into the yard
        where I dug soil
        from John's old sandlot
        soil mixed about half with sand
        that half and half with peat moss:
        then I dribbled bits
        into my finestemmed glasses

and reluctant jars
poured dabs of water in
to settle the roots
and left them to heaven

Those in Ledge Fright Seek

Those in ledge fright seek
the complacencies of the high Way
for who
given the apple of life
wants a different sweetness

    low marsh
    where water heads or sulls
    is common but
    high holdings
    marsh lofts, prevented into height,
    kept where all that can run runs,
    high marsh,
    sedge, weed, grass, tiny flower!

snow upside down and/or backwards spells
mons, the
mountainous part where snow falls
    gniwolp wons
    one of the wons

with herbicides, pesticides,
the penetration, saturation become
systemic, what for us,
the children of Mithridates's   run, the end is
poison prick   narrowing in for
    a close, the saying
midroad and midway the Way   is gaining
change, disturbance's daily loss,   concision to
shock, grief,   slash and slashing
looks illusory   slash itself off
but the world's vanishing as we
stand tiptoe at the rim of
a world never to come

water runs
but the ripple
dwells

But If the Way Will

But if the Way will
not answer common feet,
we hack through thickets,
winding vine-nodes, and
befuddling treebranching
offshooting
divisions that divide us
bringing no lessening to
the investigated material
but if like the emu we
cannot fly we can
run fast or while we scramble up
fright's sharp ledge we can
contemplate the skyWay,
treetopless, hightensionlineless,
peakless, stormcloudless
but who would be there except
as relief from here
here the pond muscles in a flash,
cracks, sprinkles, circles and
produces a disengaged item,
shining fish
delicious simmering

freedom, freedom

some people think it's going
to stop snowing
someday

today glazed because it went up
to 45 yesterday: stuff
melted and ran, and last night went
down to twenty or twenty-five:

the motion slowed, piling up, slowing,
then stopped into slick hard terrain:
today not having gone above
twenty-five, crystal-drawn
configurations, tire figurings, dry,
crunchy, are holding tight: now, forty minutes
past sundown, the dark evergreens
fall away in a white sea, clouds
above, behind, between,
only a shade lighter than
the trees:
all day the sun found two blurs
to come through, each a few seconds
wide: people who have a life
to live don't notice weather: the rest
of us study it like a feast, eating
the windshifts and coolings,
the details, main shows,
fringe events, chewing and wolfing:
who dines on clouds, drinks
the wind, gets loose mouthfuls, has
for fanfare stripped willows and
grumpy hemlocks: outriders
not regular, he should
address himself to the center
folds, vertical drapes, entryways
wherein to go straight: it is
one thing to tongue pussy and another
thing not to: well said, nature
lover: less polluted these
days than acid wind or leady sleet:

                                         the future
"let's come and eat"   will carefully
                                         husband and
Dallas at Minnesota   draw out
                                         strands of
I hope dianthus that through   the natural
platycodon simple engagement hesperis to weave the

with diverse lychnis materiality   controlled
I calendula will be able   artificial
ageratum to wipe dusty
miller the shitty salvia
grin off my cockscomb face   I need a
                                                  constellation
where all lose, one   to set a
must study gain, move into   few sharp
herd-appraisal and praise, announce   stones in
energy and direction,
not slouch behind
tempting wild animals:
        the business is serious
but wipes away,
chalk on slate, the scribbling
powdery: hunger, greed, fear,
anger write themselves out
through and with things,
then dissolve,
the things themselves also

I carry an extra
pouch on the hip, around
the neck, over the shoulder
it's awkward and burdensome,
in it a piece
of paper
with the heaviest
directive
    find
    something to save
    us, if
not a lot, a little
(tell us, at least, there
is no equivocation between
necessity and necessity)
    or if
    you can find nothing to

save us,
cheer us up
or give us a good rubdown
or put us after a problem
worth pursuing

the admiration of can-do
the basic structure
out of its holster,
admired, received—this
enlarged and multiplied
into aspects of day

hello from one who knows nothing
(and never lets you hear
the end of it)

The Sun Climbs Daily Higher

The sun climbs daily higher
into a longer arc:
lows ride
thaws in from
the south for a day or so
but the
long summer dissolve and making
this daily increment unfolds and cinches

that I	that's what I	I have to do some
take it	take it it	light writing
is what	takes	so I can do some
it takes		light reading

        taking thought

poets add
obscurity
to the
inexplicable
for critics
who can't
get their
tools sharp on
the obvious

A Seventeen Morning &

A seventeen morning &
the maple, lit below,
looks as if it's
in pearl fire
    the high-luminous snow
catching every branch
I may change rooms
because I can't see
the main subject
from here
    I can't continue
to proceed indirectly:
in the other room I wd
be able
to see a frowzy jay light in
it (my subject)
or watch a winter wind
whistle it
or behold the coming & going
of snow leaves,
nature-witnessing,
attention-getting poetry

all the fit that's news to print

what's a sphere: (you ask)
a nucleus
prowled by circumferences:
a moon or sun

or asteroid, orange, tangelo,
grapefruit, or
two selves or sexes
clustral: a mere

bead, seed, marble, an
irreducibility gathered
about itself, or a
radial awareness, more

blocked off on one side than
the other but about
as fluid and penetrating in
rock as air: awe or ire:

clearly the question is what
one does from there: the
spiral drills a more
majestic form, centralizing

spheres, binaries, clumps,
arms and windings into
vast discs turning but more
open to variety on the

edge than spheres, a malleability
outward to diversity:
moving to sweet heaps as of
rocks or garbage in spill:

every lawn,
sandy path effects, influences
the weather: every bush's
held-air temple,

cooler or warmer or more or
less humid: every fringe
of bank grass alters the
wind's rill,

spill, the way
thunderstorms roil white-ice
high with stricken
majesty: I

know how things go one
way and then the other
without separation, tenacity
continuous throughout

the measure: I
know how the big wind falls,
the winds of hollows,
thickets, ponds

adding or subtracting huff
or lag, easing or blocking,
lofting or snatching down:
clear progressions and puzzling

intermixtures: so much
stability or quiet change in
fantasies of motion: wind vane,
rain gage, barometer . . .

1 look at   2 look at
  the people   the people
  in the   in the
  graveyard   graveyard

  they   the
  don't seem to   sweet north wind
  mind

3 look at   4 look at
  the people   the people
  in the   in the
  graveyard   graveyard

  unfailing   a cardinal
  attraction   singly singing

5 look at   6 look at
  the people   the people

in the in the
graveyard graveyard

memory disturb the
slips peace

7 look at 8 look at
the people the people
in the in the
graveyard graveyard

stone recalls when dawn comes
last no one stirs

9 look at 10 look at
the people the people
in the in the
graveyard graveyard

shade quiet
trees celebration

fucking forefront
rump humper
bang spangler
wart wrestler
butt fucker shoot the breeze
people who worry about
belly wormer things have something
crawdadhopper to worry about
spider spitter
I have behind enough but
kitty cornered suffer from foreshortening
cattywompus
cattybiarsoned

diagram of eclipse
paradigm of ruin
figure of flood

                    bustnut of wind
          sketches, fit-ups for
          the cataclysm

          name and number (my culture agriculture)

          sense decays when it moves too
          far toward statement, concept,
          abstraction, or theory where
          generalization, synopsis, or
          summary has taken on wide
          prevalence but left
          behind, or digested away, any
          experience of example,
          concretion, or sensuous
          actuality; or, toward the
          coincidental, the single
          example, event, or thing
          without context or placing,
          the isolated particular:
          poetry operates, not to deny
          the abstraction or the
          particular and not to diminish
          the distance between them but
          to hold in relation the
          widest play between them

          shooting iron   today, fair, saw the sun
          don't riot bade lions   all the way down
          flowers flow   till, arc lost, it
          flower bowls   touching scattered up
                                  and down the ridge,
                                  bulbs and spherules glowing
                                  coals crumbling and I think
                                  it was 4:30 before the
                                  operation ended: this adds
                                  a minute or two
                                  to the hold of light

The First Morning in a Few

The first morning in a few
the windows haven't been
ice-befrizzled, bestreaked,
befoliaged, or befrilled,
the numerous fronds & species: today
is mostly plain
pane invisibility: but at 33
and snowing, sleeting, and
raining, a few driblets stick
to the panes still ice, clear
as ice or water, a bomb gone
off at LaGuardia
and 11 people killed:

      the snow scanty, slow,
big-flaked, I went out
into a reality
audible with unsuspected
sleet:

      round and square
          dancing and
   dancing undetermined
       square or round

I care not a fig
    for a fag in a fog
        fog in a fug
        fug in a fig
    fug a jug
      (jig a fig)

sphincter of Oddi in
your face!

it was supposed to be warm today
up to 40 or 45
but it wasn't and more sleet
fell than ice melted
now we have six new inches of
snow

This Is

This is
the great
man's skull:
we saved
it from
the fire
so you
might see
the light
in it

any part of the day you
move out of the accuracy
of honor you waste
for honor, in no need of
sanction, moves in its own
self-evidence, necessity:
    if we prove
    unworthy of tenure
    on earth earth will
    give us notice

the force of necessity
merely operates
(but lay a log across
the flow, you have
a bridge)

poison earth, eat poison

I get so much good out of my
neighbors: they don't
speak or visit
but they come

home from a trip
and put on the lights or I
look out the window on a cold
night and see one or two
of their windows lit and get
neighborly feelings

Quilted Spreads

Quilted spreads

pigeons every morning prowl
and rove
the hills at
fifty
miles an hour:
    out walking, prowling, I
hear them coming
a soft, intense muscling
then the visual speed,
cushioned rigor

constitutional

quarter to ten and the sun's
nothing, more in the south
than east,
leftover moon

are you looking for a minute,
second in the welter,
grain of what-for, nit of
news, bind of delight
    just this way

may a fart pule brown billows
about your earlobes

may your teeth acquire anal
longings and fly home

may your rump-grooving nose
plunge into the shot pot

towels pillows & bath rugs
polyester fiberfill
jumbo welt
hand-knotted fringe trim

CALL US FOR YOUR
NEW YEA SEVE GALA
an increased middle region
answers polarities
        the pode which be
            de (pod) foot and antipode
which gwine ter natcherly be
de head, baby do,
some lard, though, hung and
swung about the organs,
subcutaneous rugs, blankets,
drapes, curtains, stuffed
liver, swoll'n gut,
(with a railyard of fuming,
fussing, foaming, and verting)
these enlargements, equatorial
intensifications, of
content between the mouth
and so forth:

forget the colorless, clear,
frigid, polar life:
come to
where the   puddentang
zonky wohwoh
pleasure is

will one waft whither wind
winds forever
    the current moves with
necessity's inner accuracy
but mind what will it do
it will not accord

as if a native element
indistinguishable: it will
not have currency
but come into a state of
its own
terrain decision settles
choice disposes
some influence as to what will
and will not be
    for example choice though
will need to choose what
cannot be unchosen what is
like stone grain
    constitutional
for example loneliness
one need not look forever
out of windows or into
adjoining offices
or mailboxes
for the thing that will
not come, the face from
wax-museum memory
      no
      one may say loneliness if
with me
it is myself
it will not remove
it is mine
I hold it to myself
I will not let go of it
it is clothes on a certain
person it is a sharp watch on
a hemlock jay
it is the long tunnel of
memory personalized with
murals and hangings
it is where I must
hacking go

there will be some terror
I accept
it is mine
it comes
and when it goes
leaves furious fragrances
   one will dispose
   the disposable

I will not for example love
a new person
not with that force's full
focus
I will love sweeps, banks,
and glances
and lengthy spaciousness but
I will not
grant an extended reach
or stir to fill a need
the decision is a new knowledge,
the matter shaped and settled

monthly payment

the last day of seventy-five
some sun this morning mostly
gray this afternoon
fairly warm some melting
say thirty-five

having missed the calisthenics
of maturity
I practice early and late
to catch up with what is
gone

I am not wise
please forgive me for writing

even so
correct me with your own
deep acceptances of
condition and self
I call attention
I enliven when I can

to open press here

string out the old
string in the new

happy new year

Dung Ball, Round Graveyard

Dung ball, round graveyard,
wax ball, this sphere, nest
cell-laced with permanent eggs,
these dead moving loose
in vines through branches,
this orange body and apple body
devoured, our mouths
the substance of millings:

the sabertooth's big-game furnace
burned forty million years:
elephants, rhinoceroses stoked
it: look in his skull, cool,
polished:

the hominid ancestor dreamed
him through entanglements of fire,
the polishes of volition: the
more recent, the thinker, the banquet,
observed him go closely by:

     have you heard
     the mockingbird: those who
                            have nothing

     mark   have nothing
     the woodlark: to lose

words, a sculpture, let us
see wind:

the cart after a time
goes not on as a cart

rock the boat in a calm sea: people

in storm wildernesses hold on,
balance against, empty out,
a mindlessness resembling the
conservative: the revolutionary
is stable in it and
cannot bear it:

the upland bog!
a flat clearing
means pond-water snowed under,
and brown-shambled fringe
broken high from
by right cattails
smart and clean as pricks

    bog
    clearing
    prick freud
    ruined everything

tops in scoring and rebounding:
violence, suspense, and non-stop action:
strikes, spares, and splits:
    fireplace specialist:
    carpentry, masonry, plumbing,
    painting, roofing, wiring, heating:

            it looks like today
            though it commenced
the   a year isn't going
            to amount to much
first   gray skies
            meal-like gritty
comes   snow enough
            to make running whirls and curls
right   on the highway: we
            just went to FAYS:
after   bought a plant: the death of god

<pre>
            sort of jointy   the god of death
the   cactus put it in
            a big glass jar   cleared off late
last   had pretty good   the flat light
            roots reckon   comes underwood
if   they'll root all   like a fire
right   right the others I
before   got last week did
the
served   the content of the obsession
            changes but the form returns
</pre>

lay across the multiple
polymorphous
defining inventions
that limit and
accentuate so as to say
we, too, exist

I'm one fourth as
old as the country

I See Downhill a Patch

I see downhill a patch
mixed in the tops of two or
three cedars—the lake,
a mile's breadth hardly wider
than cedars' tips

when we dam sluices
in river gaps
we don't violate
the accuracy of flow
but build a temple
to flowing nature,
housing for the river god,
our structure interpreting river nature

time out   time up
in time   down time
            outage

yesterday the west cleared by
sunset and the sun
went down
a bright spot in an exact place
but as it went deeper
glow widened up and down
the ridge
until half an hour later
the storm had broadened
and caught up the earth
    in a rising fire

but it was only nothing
because here we are today
    (one who makes much
    of little

makes much of little
aches and pains,
trivial inconveniences,
slight delays, and is
a pain
to work with or
be around)
in a full radiance
morning having broken from
the very skin of sunrise
bright and
unrelenting and here just
past now
the windows beam,
the floor scattered with
the fallen lumber of light:
    thousands in wars have lost
their hands and/or feet—
specially in recent wars
where things picked up or
stepped on
have exploded
(if you can bear to feel it
you will never cause it)

Big Old Thang

She stuffed vulvas in the
cracks, hammered the main
labiums together with
vaginas and stapled
the clitorises up till it was
to the point he
couldn't get a thing in there.

this is your spotty reporter
folks
putting one on

first day after the first
look like it all gone down

(criticize in general
praise in particular)

The Stomach Is Quite

The stomach is quite
a development
on the esophagus and
if cross-country is
efficient
the small intestines
represent a winding
parlousness
so I don't think
we will be
concerned if the
continuo's overwhelmed
underground
by appallingly
pretentious blocks of
paydirt
it goes on trinkling under
there, eventually reappearing
enunciating

Big, BIG savings on all
units

low mileage
fully equipped
mint condition

houseflies are spongers

My Neighbor Shakes Feed along

My neighbor shakes feed along
the spruce thicket fringe and
keeps the pheasant plopping on
down, their central heating,
main ramp to life's roots:
lucky for the pheasant they
have a big ass and long
tail to sustain them above the
snow when their legs blop through

you have to feel pretty
good to have a good time:
the aspirant spiral: you remember
the aspirant spiral

the limbs' topside catches the
eye today
    high-lit with downsnow
    brighter than snow's
    underglow

the   scads
ordinary   arpeggios
realm   obbligatos
of   & cadenzas
the   of detail
ready-to-wear

(though the pentameter's heaved we're
splinter assertions of the great iamb)

Nature As Waterfalls

Nature as waterfalls,
lives, or generations
spills fast,
not fashion-fast

nature as ridge is deep
stay:
>   these the oldest
>   mountains in the
>   world,
>   authority fills the
>   clearings
>   under cedar
>   thickets

or writes precisely as the ridge
across the blue dusk coelum

authority's springs and
white-scaping falls, the responsive
rounding off of hills,
creek- and riverways
are a spelling out no
character muddles but
characters, the wind's many
motions, inscribe,
a telling not of one
thing to another, pen
to paper, chalk to slate,
skyscraper to groundbase,
microinscription to fossil
but undivided telling:
>   this writing
>   makes bowls

and fills seas: man older
than the megalith faced
unstoried stone, deep
priority, as this about here,
now after a hundred years its
millions hardly broken into:
here in America the
fashion, the scale or
intellectual sheet, sorts
against a chasm without time
and one the other criticizes
to digest but, the reach not
commensurate, the maw
can't feed: this not an
evening land but a
morning too early to make anything out:
the ridge fills our moment
and, time's fill, fills time:

there's no news like snow news:

the tongue stuck out,
tongue tip, sticky:
then teeth, mouth, the
shaping back and the business
of swallowing: the
slender esophagus, bottomed
with a valve, followed by a
great opening out, containing
another valve, then subsidiary organs,
duodenal and pancreatic, and
interpenetrated systems,
blood and air, followed by
a meandering of
guts that roil and shift,
then the water system and
larger hunks of gut (nice, necessary,
so precisely made) finally

the mechanisms of holding
and releasing

man is a motion through
variations on a tube

Larry Brown

those who fret to generate
intensity don't understand
those who thrash in lakes
of fire for the cool banks

vice versa

The Wind Picks Up Slick

The wind picks up slick
bounding upslope
on the slippery freeze

"build your own worksop bench"

insulation services
tile and formica contractor
welding
upholstery service
bath remodeling
gutter installation
heating and air conditioning
concrete construction
ceiling installations
fireplace and chimney service

the indigestible
unaired into meaning

 area rugs

saxony plush broadloom
speaker systems

  Ed White

Steelers & Cowboys

  grain off the old pebble
  pebble off the old stone
  stone off the old rock
   rock off the old boulder
  boulder off the old range

range off the old divide
divide off the old tectonic
jerk off the old jerk

arrrive

Cold Didn't Keep the Stuff

Cold didn't keep the stuff
kissed back last
fall & forsythia &
pear florets couldn't
sleep, woke up blooming
in winter's skirts

spring'll spring blossom-light

    know your onions

a sprung spring can't
unspring and spring again
till devices and
rondures have clicked
through and gone round

    ramrod concept

you would think it
easier for happiness to
happen than for
unhappiness to unhappen

    words' windy feed

in perilous times one needs
for diversion
clipped, unsustained
lyrics with no
drama (stifled cries)
vehicles to stir reality
a touch away,
to hold the unnamed nameless

back,
till when times ease one may
creep into focus on sharp
rims, the alleyways of
the long arisings
                         water
squall largely   to
shapeless   plants
the flakes   is
repeat the crystal   air
                       to
                       balloons

adultery
infantry

accomplish a designation
dense for though
we would understand   get
the world we would   this
not have it stop
or disappear

our doorstep mouse
travels little
this time of   a snow
year, waits for a dry   mole
snow and tunnels
under the surface,
a furrow burrow which
collapses behind into
permanent waves and windings,
exact histories
till high wind blows
or the sun looks

defining terms was Socrates's
way of not knowing himself

if one's hopes
cease to rise
so will one's peccadillo

I think I may not write much
today
I didn't write much before
breakfast
and during breakfast I was
busy eating
and right after breakfast
I had to go, the setting good
for getting things out but
short on things to write
them down with or on,
memory my shortest instrument:
I drove John to school, so
cold and windy,
and it took me twenty minutes
to get my pollution control
equipment overload to let up
on the choke and smoke
so I wrote practically nothing
during that time maybe a note
on a matchbook or map or
gasoline ticket (whatever,
I lost it)
so by mid-morning the time
up to then was a perfect loss
as far as writing goes
so since I had the car
already warm I went over
to the University, picked
up a few things,
arranged them, and, nothing
doing, came on back
and by the time I got the
coffee heated up began

to think of lunch
so Phyllis and I had a
great lunch composed of
soup with turkey strippings
in it, I mean we added the
turkey, it was delicious, a
delicacy, and I didn't write
a word the whole time, then
after lunch I rushed off to
be in on this thesis-defense
having to do with David Jones
and that lasted you wouldn't
believe how long
and I didn't get anything down
on paper
to speak of
but after that, late in the
day, the sun having broken out
clean into a perfectly clear
sky, I just came home and hung
in there, meditating on that
happy brightness
and as anyone knows you cannot
meditate properly if you
interrupt yourself to write
what you're thinking down
so even though we have
a quarterhour left to
sundown I don't think I'll get
much done today
                  toodleoo

Teeth Out

Teeth out   og   u
toenails in   lu   gl
                           dy   y

when you're
up you're
out of this   le mismo
world and when   difference
you're down   chickweedo
you're out   gone
                           to
                           goodness

poetry is the life of criticism

When I Think of "the Poet

When I think of "the Poet
paramount"
    how nature narrowed
    through him without
    loss of breadth

through one past the aspiration
of envy,
free of the fidgetings,
picky dispositions, effects
of lesser men (giants
themselves)
one in no need of praise
for why thank
a tree whose leaves inscribe
the sun's doings,
one better left unpraised
where praise falls away
from its object   my premature
                     sex life

entangling poet   came before
untangling critic   my mature
                     sex life

weeds don't read books
(or write them) so I sing
of weeds and they
don't turn red or pale
with embarrassment or if That
gratitude or turn me   Which Is
singing pale or red   spoke it
                     wd say
big rigs   That Which
big digs   tookus   Is speaking
bosoms

few & far between

                              when duh
when the   going git
"voice"   tough duh
(the   tough git
assimilator)   gone man
is too
strong it consumes the
particulars (words,
images, tones, meanings)
a clearing
in bulrushes as if an
elephant had paraded
through, more opaque
than voice
but no pushier

shoving every drift with oar

my poetry has   (some weeds
fallen off a   that stand
little, it has   through winter
slackened   collect
from standing   snowblossoms
right up in   bigger
there   than their summer
and doing it,   blooms)
it has weakened away,
it's soft

a hollow
log's as   ((ʘʘ))
good a   · ·
place as   ⊤ ⊤
any for
a long hole   Sigmund took our
                  head out of
                  the clouds and

gum　　　　　　hung it between
surgery　　　　our　　　legs
　　　　　　　　hello
　　　　　　　　in
　　　　　　　　there

a lot of sunshine today now falling in
gold vertical striping against
the garage and breaking to
fall on up the roof
a glorious coldness
and brightness antibacterial as saliva or vulture shit

You Can't Get It Right

You can't get it right:
if it doesn't slide off the   from side
track on one side   to slide
it will on the other or
find an unsuspected
side to slide off: it will not
go right down the slender middle
long:

stabilize political
matters by turning them
over to permanent agencies
and how do you
protect yourself against
the stability:
return the matters to politicians and,
every election re-stirring the ambience,
you lose continuity

things, tilt acquired,   he has her
achieve acceleration: all sewed up

the tongue, powerful,
moving organ, will in the
dark find bliss's button,
describe its contours,
buffet gently and swirl it,
and then swarm warmth (and
grease) into other areas
equally touchy and astonishing
suffusingly

        we are to several
        organisms, micro

and macro, in their
billions,
as islands, archipelagoes,
isthmuses, regions, elevations,
continents, seas: the mouth's
pit folks, so many kinds, the
friendly anaerobe
(honey, see your bacteriologist
twice a night)
yes
vultures (and other
       scavengers) will
eat up the ruptures, lesions, gashes,
dissolving sores of dead
animals
and gut-cleanse the disease till
shit's reductive bit, which may
stink, is (as the world
is made) pure   like so
                     so like
poets probe and punish out
dark eruptions or
invasions of the
public mind and deposit in clear
anthologies
lean germicidal turd of the just
word restored

the poet wants   the poet, torn by
to govern, sway;   maximum knowledge,
he wants   makes the best
a difficult   possible decision,
dialectical test,   tradeoff in recent
particulars forming   times—governs,
into motions and   imitating the
parties: he wants   real thing & the
contention, compromise, enterprise of each
sneak plays, judgments, of us to himself
surprises wherein he

whatever the body knows
or teaches,
the known, found through the
body, can exist other than in
the body, the dancer, for
example, the single body
never out of itself, writes
a story entangled, interlocking,
unfolded on the stage which
lasts in the head when
the dancer has gone, a rondure,
a tendency and completion,
whose composure memory finds
and forms and imagination
redisposes and revisits at will

if you could write much
superlatively beautiful
like reaches of
snow in the Rockies no
one visits
imagine high-lying
writing unread wasted on
ridges and peaks

separate as word is from
thing, the motions of the language
system correspond to
the motions of the world system
rather closely one, taking first one
and then, to the extent
possible, the other side into account,
thinks

   the woodlark,
the lilt and liquid
upward-breaking spiral,
sound's artesian spring (the

dogs get excited in the thicket
rushing up the pheasant, making
plain hens fly off
chirping) but
I love the mockingbird, childhood's
bird, most, and
weather changes or winter feed
has brought him to live here
where till this year I had
not seen him and now
with everything down white
(and mockingbird quite silent)
I see him flash across the
snow
into the big round yew or
cedar bush
whatever it is
and pick the leftover
shriveled or half-shriveled
red cedar or yew berries
and he seems fat enough
dealing with the cold long
nights (I put out a cage of
suet but he will not light on it)
I wonder when in spring
musing he'll
dropping burst the first note,
sweep a cluster of shatters into song,
and then fire the air with
a fire-line glinting unwinding

(the days lengthen, this morning's
rim-sky rosy at seven:
last evening
the great orb tucked in
a last slice at 20 to 5!)

the crow I think
has smelled my suet

but surely he
won't come to it

hanging on a nail near the
ceiling of the backporch

press the incidental
to assume the general
(any particular general)

most people don't like to think
of the stuff in their livingroom
as sitting there, chairs,
lamps, end tables, vases, tables:
they think they ought to have a focal
point, so they get something big &
noticeable, like a philodendron,
and plunk it down where nobody
can miss it
and that is not what a focal point is

     I declare the crows have
     come right in to hanging
     around in the maple tree
     and I jest bet you five
     dollars since it's over
     thirty today they got the
     scent of that suet and
     they jest a waitin' that's
     what they doin' they jest
     a waitin' sooner or later
     they gonna plunk right
     there on the porch and
     start a grabbin' and a
     tearin' well I thought this
     year I was goin' to make up
     my mind to do somethin'
     good fer nature but that

warn't the nature I meant to
do any good fer that's a
fact and I don't keer who
knows it them crows is a
eating up what little bit
of stuff people has and if
they ain't something done
about it I'll tell you they
won't be a thang left around
here that them crows ain't
fooled with I bet
you five dollars on that

see see see you can
see it for a pennis

come come	will teen wind
(unlikely)	slice the yellow
come, come	peaks off acne
(more likely)	

I have not been out to stand
near or touch the elm
recently so though I see it
occasionally through the other
room's window
I lack heavy information that
it remains substantial and yet
by faith I have no doubt
if I went out there
to hang myself on it
it would do well enough

The Perfect Journey Is

The perfect journey is
no need to go

another nothingly clear day and
I went
to walk between the pine
colonnades
up the road on the hill and there
hill-high in dry cold
I saw the weaves of glitterment
airborne, so fine,
the breeze sifting
figurations from the snow
reservoirs of the boughs

Snow of the

Snow of the
right consistency,
temperature, and
velocity will
fall in a lee
slope
building out over
space a
promontory of
considerable
reach in
downward curvature:
and snow
will do this
not once
but wherever possible,
a similarity of effect
extended
to diversity's
exact numeration

.   .   .

here a month of snow,
more January than
February, intervenes
during which
I wrote
nothing: it is
the winter-deep, the
annual sink:
leave it unwritten,
as snow unwrites
the landscape

.   .   .

The Prescriptive Stalls As

The prescriptive stalls as
to when to take effect:
the admonishment loses the
color of certainty: the
recommendation lies down like
a mule and rolls in the sand:
the traders arrive with their
incredible auctioneer and
commence to squabble
and at the end of the day
nothing has been sold or
bought: in having found no
   imbalance into a way out
   as yet, an imbalance that
   throws the leaves and
   hangings of imbalance into
   balance, I stand for
   whatever will not come round
   or be whole
   or made out or reduced:
   here breakdown allows
   the small solution to
   operate on the local problem:

this morning I got up early
and took the wetsack off my
foot, toe healing:
I went down and
turned up the heat, so
everybody could get up warm,
then I made coffee, cooked
an egg, had toast:
it was glorious enough:
but anyhow the man said it

will truly go to fifty today:
it's already 30: when all
the hills' holdings and the
trees' and ridges' loosen and
commence to trickle or
slide, gouge out and roar,
we may have a thaw
disturbance, that aspect
to happiness and warmth:
I hope it will take on
slow-moving

or after shoals of selloffs,
options, shorts, long-terms,
after heavy-risk purchases
and quick turnovers, the
unspeakable auctioneer having
fed in his energy and taken
his toll, there at the day's
end is my portion: crust:
    I just got back from the
University: so many
matters of great interest and
no moment:
but in the moment the general
world assigns,
    the special person, the
    one taking the brunt,
finds the ultimate explosion:
a former student, now
representing a book publisher,
stops by: he is engaged:
soandso calls that soandso
will not keep the appointment
because her father has died:
    soandso left her dog
    at home shut up
    because he runs after

bitches and winds up
  in the pound:
a University writes offering
me a job: one who
wants to apply for the job
won't get it:
          the turn of the day:
          the spill, waterfall, shed:
impossible to make
any version
(perversion better than no
version at all)
adequate to the circumstance:
one enlarges the scope
and increases the fill-in:
deepens, dumps, delineates
the fill-in:

who or what is watching over
the waterfall (the waterfallwatcher)
where the
spill picks up, the urgency   we can be okay
takes on muscle and speed,   socially and
the fast overshoot with   know that the
giddy, weightless fall,   same moral laws
and the splintering disturbance   are operating
against bottom, rock, water: as before, as
things pick up, of course,   usual, and still
from there and go on in a new   grind crudely at
mildness but strange setting: the circular
some things pass into   edge between
unrecognizable strangeness: human and natural
   is no one watching, of   law, one harmony
   course not,   not disclosing
      not even a gentle, universal   how it
principle with a calming circularity,   meshes with
a soft persuader reminding us   another
of the marvels, the high   harmony
concerns and yearnings over

us, the realms luminous our
understanding
need only bend for comfort to:

are we here, single things,
lifted up into clarity and
recognition
by the same powers and forces
to be struck down, the calm
coasting going quite on beyond
us: or is it here precisely
that sleeve enters sleeve
so we see the interpenetrations,
to live to die, not to
die not to live, this is
the motif, announcement,
deep conditioner, the knowledge
from which there is no
freedom and no freedom
except in the knowledge,
the hardest, most bitter
schooling beauty and decay
could have devised,
allowing, though, ironic sweets
highest invention is humbled by:
   one is helpless: one weeps: e
   terror raves beyond the tear: q
   one is without help: u
   and then one sees or recalls   a
that on the balance line between n
purchases and payoffs   i
indifference looks neither this   l
way nor that:
our help is the call of
indifference that says
come where there is no
need of help
and have all the help you need:

so we rock (and roll) between gratitude
and terror (burns the cheek)
so we commend ourselves to
what is to be and what must be
so we celebrate dome's day, the
big theatre, we came to see
and so we quail
at show's end, the going back
into forgotten dark,
the stripping off of illusion's privileges:
the sleep beyond the
edge of the deepest sleep

my fears of the
piling up of too
much fluency
in high-rise temperature were,
I think, ill-founded
for though the radio says it is
now 42
the drips from the garage eaves
slow winter down:
you could write a sonnet
between one drop and the next

insecurity of registration in
a terrain measures the
potential, that susceptible
to disposition or re-disposition,
but to the extent that potential is pure
potential, with not a skimming
of announcement or definition,
it is nothing, who needs
potential: and yet who does
not, not need "give", border
or boundary stone

relocateable: if you could,
for example, set poetry off
into 10 orders of this and
that, subsidiary systems spelled out, lifted into
interpenetrative connection
with what is perceived to be,
you could call it preserved
territory, a public or private
garden, identity certain:
but poetry resists this, yielding to erosion,
horse manure, bird droppings,
pine needles, the wind, moss,
bracket, bract, stone of change,
a troublesome, marvelous garden:
fertility inexhaustible, a milling:

After the Dissolve

After the dissolve,
under cedars and black and blue
spruce,
hemlock thickets,
crescents of coverless
ground where
if pheasant eat grass
pheasant can
plick chilly uprights of
green grass
or sort through the
vegetal remains, rubble for seed or
seed-like knobs,
clusters, or pods, roots, or
whatever
contributes generating to
the possible: but now
my class over for today
traces of white airiness
mean-sprinkling are expanding
into hard lightness
again, temperature falling,
new snow on old
melt-rinsed-to-ice snow

    limited visibility
    yield ahead
    yield
    stop
    frost heaves
    merging traffic

                    at most dusk
bill of goods   the ringneck
deepdown clean   as if reluctant

I saw enough   to fly up to roost
of the real   walks about
to flee and   on the meltshade
found enough unreal under the cedar,
to return to   his feet on the
see the real   ground for the first

time since midDec: he walks elegantly,
slowly, now and then bends
to peck:
of course, he sleeps
on warm legs and feet
but all day every day he's
snow-plopping barefooted:

scouring ugliness
and bathing beauty

my friend the   drover
   poet is no   oversold
longer attracted   oversoul
to any   lover
   center of which   mover
he is not   shover
the attraction

A Sift, Sprinkling, or Veil

A sift, sprinkling, or veil
of snow came
last evening sun after dusk
but ended soon:
today, though, is bright!
I got up at 6:30 to turn up
the heat and the
east was brightening: oh,
I said, the sun may come up
this morning and now it is
bursting pointblank against
the thicket

Structureless Rage, Perhaps

Structureless rage, perhaps,
pure energy of motion, volition, lies
alongside or moves under
and upfloats appetite: blah, blah:
an energy that we should have
been put here among these   one with no
bounties and possibilities,   community has
crippled with these walls and only the world
spoons:
    rage then flares into fear
that resentment has destroyed
our chances with the good
makings, the father dispraised:
    it is a circumstance
medicine cannot surround or
work preservingly to the core
of: we must be and be
destroyed at once: rage and
love, fear and love, these
work themselves
out so that we become
accredited lovers and fearers
with no loss to either wing:
with no cancellation into
boredom or indifference:
harsh: harsh: with the
fate-like calm acceptance
that no other mix could keep this stir:
          in a bush's
          fine division
the sparrow lights free
from the hawk's broad shoulder:
          tie one on:

another matter:
there is not
at the moment   y
one single flake   e
of snow on   a
the garage roof:
a warm day again up to 45,
good old February
and there are wide circles
of dark ground under evergreens
and oblongs and funny
strung-out clustral darknesses
under groves, along hedges,
the woods in untouched natural color
but it's gray again   .
    (it's gray again
      like clay again!)

uyyl lggu ugyu lygl
glug yuly yllg guuy

Tell What Will Not Tell Direct

Tell what will not tell direct
encompassingly:
the bindings of avoidance
gather terrain
manysided and cushioning,
should the direct route of
the direct saying emerge,
should the furrows of
circumference, hills
and dells, the wild,
off-the-mark talk,
lead to the very place unspoken
standing out where the stand
must be taken,
avoiding avoidance

    go out of your
      out of your
   way to help
     others
      help others

but watch it what you raise into
strength may suspect you of
strength withheld and raid you
down and out loose, windy

since before day
and all day
the wind's rolled billows across
us, the soundlessness,
rising roar, crash,   weave is what it is:
muffling, sucking   no matter the wisdom,
against the house   perception: the truth,

and this
with the sky gray gray as
before as usual
well but even so it's good
weather for February

great weather's
destruction, though:
the blue dry high
radiant inanition
shrinks brooks to crisp
routes
burns grass
upholds dust

yes, but only because
attendance to truth
enlarges complexity:
but is one wave of the
weave blanced by an
equal & opposite: that
is important: is
everything stressed but
in its proper place:
is consideration
observed in the
dispositions: not an
ailing net but
adequate weave

find reality
find duplicity
two bows of a single knot

my feelings are caught
gauze in a strong wash

with the prevailing snow
and full moon
nothing prowls through here
at night
without prowling declarations

raccoon prissy
used sway

Spread It Thin

Spread it thin
zip it in

give me a ring
    go back up for a lay
        (better laid than never or up)

today continues the tropical
extravaganza—up to 45,
the circle of under-cedar melt having
widened halfway across the
yard and the pheasant pecking here &
there significantly

an interim free of spring
madness and summer dangers
a protectorate of warmth
midway winter's wars

bees body cells of the animal, hive

today you couldn't get a sprig
of hemlock to wiggle
where yesterday
bounding sloped green
surfs
permanent as breaking
entanglements: when the wind
does not arrange to have
tongue, much is tongueless,
as great distance

Dark Day, Warm and Windy

Dark day, warm and windy,
light breaking through
clouds
coloring the sides of tall
furrows, thaw decaying
snow, the wind stirring
time up to a rush, I come home
from work midmorning
dark with contemplations,
   that the infant finds
   his hand unopened
   and the old man forgets
   his has closed—that rondure:
I sit down at the piano
and try the "Fuga 1" in *The
Well-Tempered Clavier* and
my feelings lighten,
the melody so incredible,
the counter-melody incredible,
the workings in and out
precise and necessary

Like Fifty

Like fifty
I'm fifty

      ditch water,
      spring caterpillar,
      ripples downhill,
an eager
thermometer,
the volume of motion a direct
reading of melt
and melt keyed to the temperature

so during the time of thaw
correction made for
shrinkage of reservoir,
the ditch
with some variable constant
lag tells:

I don't care much about the
language these days (!)—turn this upside
                  down and you have
      I want   the happiness
to make a point: without measure
the point is essential,
the connection: the language
should be adequate:
(I've felt, might as well admit
it, other ways (not
necessarily opposite (
sometimes opposite) ways)
before)

if mush were slush   dud
meep could sleep   dad

scruffy lines between me & my
neighbors, lean thickets,
spirea brown fine-bush and
overhangings of maple, silver
and sugar, big spruce,
honeysuckle bush-stump, ground
cover, and my own kept ant
hills: stringy wilderness
inhabiting civilization's
straight lines

a half-century inscribed
birthday cake, promises
of presents, a wheelbarrow
(red, rained on) and stereo!

A 41 Morning, Still Cloudy

A 41 morning, still cloudy,
rainy, gray, vague, the only
snow left
skinny archipelagoes, once
drifts, or stalls, as by (before)
(or after) garages or thickets:
   the forecast is for
    skin temperatures dropping
    through the day
    into snow flurries
with no significant
accumulation:

   still three months away to leaves:
   for us now there
   is a discontinuity in the
   flow of energy from the
   physical which we still can
   trust some to the metaphysical
   now exploded: ideally, the
   physical would be the roots
   or trunk and the metaphysical
   would arise easily and smoothly into
   the subtleties of embranchment
   allowing, when leaved, flows
   and wavings of light, variable
   shades, tones and atmospheres
   like the spiritual temper of a time:
   for us now, we dig in to
   see if the trouble with the
   boughs is not some trouble
   with the roots and so we have
   nearly killed the tree:

still, however long it is to
leaves, the grass has from
this warm spell taken
the hint, sprung its leaves
up into the cushions of air
and given out a tint hint:
imagine, the readiness
of it all! the unwearying readiness
to cycle, eagerness all over
fresh, as if for the first time:

now the tree is cracked off
at the ground: a peel of
cambium holds the boughs:

the boulder columns
of the temple
    hold
up (arbor-skinny
roof)
eternal emptiness

I brought in the garbage
cans, there was
(at this temperature)
a faint smell in them:
it was
nearly pleasant:
    spring's first
    midwinter
    fragrance:

we eat the dead, swirling decay into
such a fret it gives energy off
to us, saprohumanists:
we can't go on long eating and shitting and
beshitting the world before,

eaten, we are beshat:
the banqueter's the banquet:
(well, then, dine!)
look you to it:

will not the wolfer be wolfed:

can there be a dwelling for man
with no cock to cry the days
in: I hear from across the lake
in quiet spells
dogs barking or crows cawing: or,
even, though terribly early,
geese going over, high over:
in any case, it is not the
rooster, wing-thubbing and crowing:
do you not miss the biddies:
yellow butterballs
peeping about the hen's legs
and beak:
do you dwell securely where
there is no cackle to the lay
    and no offal dog neither
    nothing
good Lord not even a guinea:
I need pig and fowl: company:
and the goat!
how I need a goat!
what is the flavor
of anything without
the bright-eyed,
astonished,
big-balled billy: or the
fucking sheep: who can do
without it: what we have is
    the radio blaring
    a flat high level

of disaster this
and disaster that:
when I lived in the world
there was nothing worth doing
doing

Produce and Fuctifry

Produce and fuctifry

a snow so misty, melty,
and thick
only careful looking sees it:
it does not resemble itself
on garage or grayass: my
    teeth and victory stick
    dream of being
    hard on
    cavities

guys with things so fine
they consider noses
or so blunt   (earful,
they blunder ears   getting an)

stuprum   stream   new snow
stupulose mill run   on old
           wash   melt narrows
           brook   brooks
           creek
           branch
        mill race
        mill
        mill town
        mil town
        Mil ton
        Milton

geese did fly over yesterday!
northward along the east shore
harkking & honnking
in the accustomed ways:

seeing believes even if belief
can sustain seeing

an inch of snow fell during the night
drawing lines in the trees and
filling bushes with snowberries, big ones,
fork blossoms
                              at least
                              more fell
                              than rose

I Look Up Guff and Find the First

I look up *guff* and find the first
thing I learned about Babylon, the
gufa, the round wicker boats
in the fourth-grade reader! and I
remember the camels slinking high
against the flat, low line in the
background
with the aerial twist of leafage
at the palm top:
I can taste the sand now that I could
taste then, the muddy yellow river,
I feel the gristy hot soup of it now
that I did then!

    mean business

the split between us

snow remains (remains
of snow) out under
the woodsedge brush
        and lee of the put-out
        Christmas tree, there a dab
        (white scab)
and up here before the big yew
which brought the wind
paused to a crescent fall-out

histories of past
motions thawing away into motions,
runlets and trickles,
histories of redispositions

I cry nothingness nothingness as long

as the inadequate, the issuistic, is
proposed: I cry nothingness nothingness
to open space for the more nearly
adequate should it be deeply spoken for or of:

the dialectical
sways
in on the clarification of
oversimplification
and falls in to opposite or
indifferent tendencies:
and after heavy losses on both sides
burns itself out in error and
grief and astonished self-correction
only to go a little way
too far the other way,
take on concentration,
force, and direction,
lean down into an assertion
that challenges, tests others
and then the opposite sway
falls into motion
with heavy losses, etc.
        nothing achieved apparently but excuses
        to form energies idly potential, test
        belief, swell the capacity to tolerate tragedy:

the economies, the allowances and costs, are so
finely adjusted, broadly and thoroughly applicable,
it is hard to believe the absurd design, haphazard:
though it would be dialectically just for economy to
be grounded in happenstance because only at the level
of absolute freedom of bit could swells of new
information rise to alter the valuations of the economies

the weather today continues
recent trends: 35 at dawn,
near 40 now at 10:37 a.m.,

supposed to go maybe to 45:
high for tomorrow 40:
the tiger lilies are green
nubs standing in ice:
I see a hollyhock leaf
or so lying on the ground,
still green, the snow cover
having kept it :they say
there are snowdrops up
(a switch from the downs) and
crocuses are heaving off
shelves and roofs

One at One with His Desire

One at one with his desire
slurps not the bone soup
of syllables
    but rises to the other's
    rose and falls immediately
    from
feeding desire
to recollection or anticipation
of desire
    the business of the day
    not bending the contour
    out of circle

one not at one with his
desire has not a whole
intention
    and consequently no place
    to go unqualified
    or any single thing to
look for but one aspect
of himself knows the
otherness of another aspect
    so that he cannot become
    disentangled
    into other otherness

all singers are blind, of course,
for the same reason that they
do not see the world
    but thickets of
    complication between
    themselves and their desire:
so much loss for the little
rescue of a lilt, a passing

fine turn, a modulation
   practiced and true:
   art's
   nonbeing's

dark consolation:
what a nice stanza! imagine just going
on: I think I've invented
   rooms to walk through
   or stand amazed
   or lie sleepy in:
it is no place, though,
to rehearse the flesh
of the beloved,
   it is no place to touch
   or taste
   enter or leave:

it is dry delight, whatever
service remains when
the church closes:
   the sweepstakes of
   no desire
   whole as fulfillment:.
the sweetest passer of time
scheduled for emptiness:
the drug that makes erasure
   bliss: an illusion some
   of the uneasy can cover
   misery with:

still when you think of the
nourishment of such delight as
over starvation,
   what a numb pale
   paradise! how constant
   the music
dwelling among the constant

bushes, the deathlessness only
lifelessness can know
    one not at one with his
    desire still has to desire
    so much more than nothing

        this stanza compels
        its way along: a
        break will humble it:

        form consumes:
        form eliminates:
        form forms the form
that extracts of the elixir from
the passages of change:
well, we mustn't let this
        form reverse itself
        into an opposite
        though parallel
largely similar insistence:
must we?

a marvelous morning
dull gray aflood with the possibility of light

live unknown!
(the protean density   a pane's
of that!)   mirror
unmonitored by   lets
the clichés of praise   everything
                        through

well, no, the light changed
away into indistinguishable   if you froze
gray, flicking wet dashes,   a fog, that's,
gravity-sprung ellipses, on   turned loose on
the windowpane: a bluster, how
colder, foggier, suddenly: snow-fine's
a front entering us doors   the stuff today

//
we have become now in
the afternoon balled up
horizonless in pearly
mist, a billion bits of snow
jostling this
way and that, coming
down and putting
differentiation down downy:

the temperature dropped
in an hour twenty degrees an hour
an hour

sheet-deep in sleet
        I haven't written as
        many words as an hour's
        grains of sleet
and so far only a scattering
impression of white
has risen from the lawn:
one should go on till one's
hue is
unmistakeable

nature goes so far to make
us one of a kind
and treat us all alike

Dull Lull

Dull lull
palustral
mule
logging a
swamp   sull
pompous
ramps
amperage
palatial
labial
mull
gulls

dropped to eenzie teens last
night and snowed
three inches
now at noon it's
the biggest teen

the car was crunchy and
crusty with
frozen rain in the windshield
wipers, stuck,
and the door wouldn't break
open and every window was
snowed white,
tribulation's Parian wreaths
(hark, a footnote)

hurdygurdy hurlyburly
loveydovey

with the snow white
as snow and the light

bright as day
one sees too much to see
outside
//1:50 p.m.
though it is
warm by the
window and though
the garageroof snow
cannot but melt
and tinkle twinklefree
at the eaves
still the thermometer
has not budged up a bit
all day
standing right where it
is regardless of what-all
the sun pours it on day
and (elsewhere) night
but the air masses will come
variably from here and there
and they warm and cool in
cycles longer than a day
longer than a week maybe
even longer than a year
as long maybe as the 11
year sunspot cycle or
sunspot cycles well
you get the point
just because you
have a fair day you
can't expect the
temperature to
shoot right up
to seventy like
I told this
writing
student of
mine who

                        was a real
                        tomato
I said you don't say to a
tomato you just set out make me
a tomato you say to it
make leaves and stems and
roots and branches, acquire
an abundant presence, and
then easy as pie you will be
able to make lots of tomatoes
and I think this girl got the
point that a Platonic form is one
thing and a piece of ass
something else
and nobody with that kind of
awareness will stay puzzled
long or talk to teachers
queer for tomatoes

enough horse do for today
ltho prhps ct shrt

The Temperature Rose 15 Degrees over

The temperature rose 15 degrees over
the sunless, unaided
night: clouds like freight
cars packed the heat in
here and like tarpaulins
held it in place: high
winds today will change the
pacings and placings, only to add heat
to heat: high

    winds shake out from scruffy
    snow-disorganized bushes
    crosslimbs, tangles, and
    dead twigs and comb every
    long branch out into its
    separate space and possibility,
    a ruffling and swaying
    that brings cleansed motions
    to high alignment!

rhythm is the spreading out
of sense so that curvatures
of intonation, gestures of
emphasis, clusters of
relationship can find disposition
and placement within the
enclosing identity of the sense scope
                (as metrics eats
                away at motion
                it loses its identity
                and becomes like motion)

metrics aside, though (and
why not, though relevant) much
of the power of motion resides

in the reliability (see dict.)
of the repetition (al fine
senza repetizione): at some point
in the whole
scope of an act
of congress, encouraging
trust, there ought to be a
plateau, a plateau before the
peak: it needn't be a flat
plateau: it can be building
at an angle into buoyancy:
but for this part of the act,
a regular rhythm or a regular
progression (generally
accelerating) ought to be
established as the highest
feeling comes on stressful
entering or unstressful
withdrawing: but aside from
the regularity of duration, timing,
between stresses (c'est a
decir, a poem or novel must
achieve identifiable motion
as the highest contour above
its many motions): it follows
from the reliability of these
stresses and durations that
the pleasures that lie ahead
are available, can be reached,
ought to be entertained:
reliability gradually
accelerated could then explode
into huge releases of, umm,
expression, into dissolving,
stressless gliding, unwrinkled
calm

expression through issue   creelo o no
is not too bad   creelo o yes

if clusters of plurality
balance counterbalances:
that way, all expressions
are tolerable but
meaningful change is slow,
an undercurrent forming past
calculation in accuracy:
                the unwilled will
                will the future
                more truly than the
                willed will:

10:10 a.m.: it has cleared
up sunny and warmed to the thirties:
the snow's not rushing into melt
but clumps have damp edges: one thinks
the buds and flower-clusters
have swelled but actually one
has only thought of spring
and noticed the buds for the
first time: they've been about
so big all winter:

                prey bolts, whines
                but overtaken is pulled down,
                dignity of design
                forgotten in dust and the
                fastest heart beat, grace
                of motion
                broken down into dinner

(have so many things to do that you
rarely do them)

//5 p.m.
my first walk to the brook
this year and though
it was only 15 minutes

including taking out the garbage
it was exhaustingly delightful
   the brook by the way
   by the way ay ay
   is sassy
   up to roaring
   the water melt-muddy with
   road runoff (salt, ash, cinders,
   & gravel) and cutting gullies:

good to see a streak of water oozing
in caterpillar ripples across
the dry highway and to notice
farther up
the forsythia thicket letting its
holdings of groundsnow go

I would love to get the poetry just
the way it happens, the way it comes
on, heavy and thick like
a thunder tangle or empty as high
blue, weaving, stalling,
a little bit of all the
progressions including the
unstirring:

   hunt   high
   wild   ass

on the walk a fart worked its
way loose
probing through like a variable
long balloon seeking
till
wind to wind it broke free
so generous & satisfying

As for Fame I've Had It

As for fame I've had it
before I've
had it: meanwhile,
others grow vast on
very little
   (but it has
   by wise men
   often been
   spoken: less is
         more or
         less more)

while the more
I give the fewer
tangles of
attention to me
unwind

I suppose I've
worried too much
about the outbreak
of destructive
clarification:
when most folks
are in such confusion
any slight light
falls into far illumination

in darkness will we
heed too much
the twinkling of a tiny
twinkler when on the
mountain
chasms, gulfs, ravines,
ledges and weighty slides wait:

to be made of steel!
so bullets and aches and
pains and sorrows
the sorrows of knowing and
not knowing and witnessing
bing off you
that would be so fine
provided you did not
remain stiff and
uneducated

meanwhile the day has been
beautiful from sunlight binging
right off the horizon
through bright to now 3:15:
not as warm as yesterday but
warm enough, 40, 45:

poetry has become an outing
(outage), church social, a picnic of
huggy self-embracing, small hopes
and a tremendous capacity to bear
up under daily disappointment,
no mail, no state funds, no
fed funds, no city or county
funds, no scholarship or fellowship
today, no
subsidy on this issue, no
programs for the public
or public schools this week, no
improvement at all, I'm sorry,
we can't offer you a
reading engagement this year,
no, not now:

take up slack
choose cheese

When One Is a Child One Lives

When one is a child one lives
in helplessness, in terror
of arbitrary force, and in the
fear of death

when one is young one lives
in helplessness of the
passions, in terror of the
ultimate vulnerabilities, and
in the fear of death, passion's
opposite

when one is grown one lives
in helplessness of the webs
of demand and responsibility,
in terror of failing, and
in the fear of death, the temptation

when one is old one lives
in helplessness, in terror, and
in the fear of death

a windy, almost flashingly
changeable morning, the
clouds ripping across
influxes of light, that moist
blue in the clouds, temperature
50 but failing, the willow
yellower, perhaps, than
usual, or more noticeable
against the rank clouds

instability is a loss into
motion but the best integrities
move, the coming out
of "sense" from sound
progressions: the
"flow" on the court to a swish:

    crows sit in the thicket
    hushed mainly in the noon
    cloudiness:
    when the great geese
    fly over
    the crows appear strange
    as if separated into their
    contemplations

most anything, stopped, falls
apart: motion
is the world's glue
   holding-together
but time eventually underslips
the whole thing

it is so lovely, the world,
so full of change and death
   how can we find ease
   in the uneasy
   stability and calm
   in the rushing
   where is our stay
   that is in a holding
   higher
   than motion's formings

here, we know a stillness that will
not work, and, there, a
stillness we can't stir from:

hold on to your self and your things
as long as there is
hope of holding: then swirl
loose into the mercy of others, set
your sights on having nothing,
staying nowhere: rest home:

who lets go needs not even
the need to hold on
he is free with nothing
which is in to everything,
these strange and comforting
contradictions, emollients,
ointments, and
soothing sanctions for the lost:

swashbuckling bushwhacker

the weather cooled and calmed
into 4 o'clock
sunny, nice

I look out
the window   bang bang
but the only   yr're dead
thing coming   brush your teeth
is another   and go to bed
tooth out

      if I had   language says
      more fight in   wise and
      me there   sobering things
      would be less   but in
      run   real binds
                            nobody reads

I picked up lost wood under   sores run
the elm yesterday afternoon   scabs
limbs airy with light rot   stay put

bark expanding to separate
speckled white with decay

high winds trim the tree
into the continence and
security of calm
                    frijolillo

Cloud Strays Rounded Up

Cloud strays rounded up
in a windy direction before
dawn, a hustled, rustled
    clearing

as the stone buildings at the
university get older
life seems more and more
like whitewater over an
architectural rapids

    slope soak
    seeps (spews up)
    through a
    highway chuckhole
    late at
    night and
    freezing through
    early morning
    builds up ice
    which
    when dawn brings out
    the cars
    grinds fine
    under the tires
    and looks
    like a bucket
    of dumped
    gook

a curiosity to pedestrians admiring
the sunny morning

newlyweds: honeyback guarantee

can your father stuff it

the Rangers can't
seem to do
anything in their
own end
something outside the bedroom
maybe a shutter
burrs in gusts and
another thing, an electrical
attachment, squeaks at the
corner of the house as if
someone were squeezing
a bird or turning over on a
spring

(at nigh on to three the wind
has died down but the
temperature has gone right on up to
sixty)

tulip leaves are up
green spears of lilies show
an inch of daffodil is
up
the hollyhock clump that was
aleaf under snow
having lost those leaves now
to naked frost
has unfolded held small leaves
precaution freed from caution

maybe the Lord troubles
peoples' knees so they
will pray short and get on
with what must be done
//it's getting late &
we had a shower

(enough to lay the salt
and silt on snowroads):
Bernie's coming to dinner & Don
couldn't quite get the
backboard up on the face of
the garage and I have pulled
out old spirea stalks and
picked up sticks till I'm
pooped nevertheless let's see
if we can approach the
brushpile principle: now
a brushpile is by nature a
place to throw things
but you must be careful
when you throw armloads of
this or that on the pile—
some pieces will slide
down and off the pile or you
will dribble a stalk or so
of something just before you
get to the pile
    which is only to say that
    in normal usage
    you will start to blur the
    line between the brush pile
    and the periphery
this should not be permitted
because pretty soon you'd be
kneedeep in junk before you
could get to the pile with a
load: right:
principle: be sure to police
the periphery of your fucking
brushpile
or you will wind up with
nothing but a mess,
an undifferentiated junkyard:
is that what you want:

do you want that:
    lines sometimes help the mind
    take steps from
    one thing to another
    possibly ascending steps
    to the tall place
    where nobody
    walks around

leap year

It's Half an Hour Later before

It's half an hour later before
a spring shower
gets all the way down
to hemlock ground

last night it rained easy
all night till dawn the rain
got white and
the dawn world, stained this
or that, came up white
coming up on white

they's a limit, he said:
she cracked up,
    mother nature's response
    to male weaknessdomination

and all morning up to now
heavy stuff, white and sticky,
right on the rain line,
has been falling in a
calmness no tree quivers

winter trees aren't good
winnowers: nevertheless
fine branches snatch flakes
and big branches take
single ridges: the chaff
    hits the ground
    but the caught
    turns to lit melt beads
    that light up
    trees in a different light:

march one and	march	one and
in the clear	in the	clear
thicket highchoired	thicket	highchoired
grackles grate squeak,	grackles	grate squeak,
dissonant as	dissonant	as
a music school	a music	school

not much verse today but we
got the backboard & hoop up

This Poem Concerns

This poem concerns
the elm over past
the windows of the other room

the elm includes the weather

this poem is largely about
the weather because
weather is a major influence
on elms

you've heard I know that the dutch elms
are gone
this is to remind you
that they are still gone

                       but I heard
we come from up   a man once
to 30 billion yrs   whose thing
of oblivion but think was done and
of not even a   whose race
little more lightly   run say
                       he was ready

the great flash their selves
onto, obliterating, surroundings:
they are normal:

cutting back, undercutting, schools
us to lessenings, including
the total lessening, nothing:

from what bin more gigantic than stars
could the diet be doled:

doled! poured out!
when the biggest thing, the grand repository,
we have is oblivion, slick with emptiness

will the fed few
feed on
cut-aways
from the schooled starved

we applaud the loudmouth who
breaks through into the feast of our portion!

could shed your shingles
could shingle your shed

today was a fair day all day
and most of the snow got
mopped up except
here and there next to
trees, fences, in thickets
hard to get at

I turn to the word and it brings me
anything:
I no longer go to look about in the world:
I have become so lonely
that only the word
is free enough and large enough to take my
    mind off
    the world going day
    by day over the brink
    used up but unused:
how thankful I feel
bent gutless over
the vomited void
to have at least the word
going anywhere fetching anything:
pretty soon it may have

brought so much
it will not need to go off again
and then the word will
draw me up about it

The Word Cries Out

The word cries out
and I fetch

a thing or thought is noted
and from need or in
response to pressure
    urgency for a verbal version arises
and words dash in
taking trial positions,
sort and re-sort themselves   wor(l)d
into provisional clusters
and whole strings:
    a marshal, severest linesman,
shouts out down the ranks
and ta-tum
the verbal version
with last minute stumbling or twitching
on the edges
declares itself   there was a heavy
its trimmest   frost of snow on the garage's
                             roof scales but the sun
I hunt and peck   wiped it off
leaf through   or the garage crawled away
check alignment
do it again
start over
wait a while
look up
reconsider, readjust:
friendly word, image,
you hold my attention:
even as attention fails
and revives with work,
stirring and re-doing:

now as many snowflakes as you would find
bees working a quince clump, flakes big
as mayflies, run or stall or turn or rise
in the wind all together, flocks, swarms,
droves of things: this may be where fish
got the notion of turning in a single
action (it snows over oceans)

I Woke Up at 6 and It Was

I woke up at 6 and it was
light enough
to shell peas or water begonias:
midwinter, fine-work would
have had
to wait till eight:
    two days off from spring,
two hours of light
attached to both ends of the
day, the middle position
will enlarge, going on
to four hours either end,
sixteen dark switched to
sixteen light:

the reason it makes
no difference what people
think
is that they don't think
enough to make any
difference

the weather got us this week:
Tuesday an alldayer, a
heavy snow with the temperature
dropping, dropping (from the
shales of the morning) so low
that last night, low teens,
jungle escalations, ropes,
vines, fronds, seized the
windows crystal-blind again:
        today
        the sun came up
        in light,

to warm to thirty: that will do
in the garage snow (an inch
on the windy side, one to three
inches on the hemlock side):
yesterday at the university as, my
wont, I mused out my window,
I saw a certain twist and
horny warp
registered in the deep-long
eaves icicles and since
Tuesday night had been windy
I thought, my word, icicles
summarize the rate of melt
and wind direction, are a glacio-spiral
version of a wind-rose: nature
that will uproot an eavesload
of history
can be so careful of history

A Flock of My Days

A flock of my days
either gone already or to
come rises up
in a flurry and flies into
itself
setting off
a maelstrom descent, whirlpool bloom
with a fine hollow stem figuring for a
bottomless source

in yesterday's dusk hickory,
a flicker black on skylight,
not a grackle but a
    robin! the behavior exact,
    year's first!
pecking his breast, grooming,
regarding the groundcover of
snow unsharply
(but today the temp is to go
to 60, worm raising weather)

yesterday when melt was
commencing late
in the afternoon
one icicle with a fringehold
on the eaves
waved back and forth
windily
as if hinged,
its hold become so light

but now this morning
the temperature nearing fifty
the eaves rain with
melt, rooftiles starting to show

radiance's darkness
(too much light on too much snow)

I guess the lady next door
when she had the elm thinned
from the thicket
didn't know
snow would cap a hemispheric cone
on the left stump

they say it took some days
for the cries in No Man's Land
to die down: first
  there was a noise
  of pain
  but a few dawns and dusks
  settled things
down to here and there
a filament of dissent
and then the dawn came wherein
the peace was incredible

You Can't Imitate

You can't imitate
anybody really
and the extent
to which
you can't is
enough originality

the extent to
which you can't
imitate anyone
really is enough
originality

one gains
with immortality
a lasting
tomb

after another blow
I pick up
loose wood
under the elm,
hard branches, the
skinny bones
of a flesh

if you caught a
dusk-glimpse
as a first seeing
of the thin-tapering
hemlocks (a row
of raving beauties)
you'd think they'd,
waggled and whipped,
worn off in the
wind that way

left
that was leaves

ringneck &
redwing
(redneck &
ringwing)

Stevens, you should be here
now with the ringnecks
and rigorous rednecks
and the green billows
of grass with drained
hunks of black-old
snow floating in them
and the ringnecks
stirred by a nosey dog

racing into the thickets!
if you could hear the
brook like a bear breaking
through the thicket

(the thicket floor
a manuscript patches
of snow illuminate)

yours truly
yours treely

    "live unknown" is
    no fun unless
    you have to work at it

why kill
yourself when
you can
die
without
your help   trees fall to
           the wind
           and falls'
           murmuring
           trees the wind
the comet mingling
with us this
week (a
windy week)
will
be back in
fifty
thousand years   the grave may
           not be its
           goal but that's
           where it lands
the world's too serious

to take seriously &
too funny to take lightly   faint &
                                          fall over
Old Milling

say to the race
your run's
run its race

say to the run
your race's
race's run

Spring's Old Hat Is Older

Spring's old hat is older
than hills:
but spring's skinny shade
(as old)
gives cedar, pine, spruce,
upstart and low-profile,
the jump on maple,
elm, latecomer

my yew ball
is ten feet high and wide
(it doesn't roll in
but unrolls the wind)
you can stand behind it
when there're insistent breezes
and it's like standing
on the bank of
a current and even if the wind
is sucky
blowy with variability
the whole
context
is diminished in a matrix
of holding

The Temperature Fell

The temperature fell
through yesterday afternoon:
big clouds came
and winds rose: and fell
and the clouds came and went
and the temperature fell on
through the night
plunging into the teens
from a daytime high
above seventy

today though the sun is out at
times and
though the wind, steady,
has lessened,
the temperature is staying
where it fell,
snowflakes feeling
their way (more
numerous than far-off legions)
through the air
in fabrics too fine for "snowing"

goalless as a ping
pong table I'm
as a free-versite
also netless
(courtless)

systems, structures,
big hunks of culture
do not melt and flow
directly
one to the other but

  turn
  articulate
  dis-poise
often on single glints of
perception,
the exception sharply noticed
become the groundwork
of the next familiar:
  as one who looks
to the mechanisms and costs
(sad joy
breaking away into acceptance)
in the "flow" of systems and
structures
I cannot stop to see if
at any point a thing
still moving was
satisfactorily complete:
the sky's stabiles
hasten and churn:
  I befriend, or hope to,
gently,
motion: it is my slow veracity
and belief:
the conveyance of discard is
the arising of beauty:
perception, flat, impersonal, out-of-context
perception disfamiliars, erupts motion:

  my life (pent)
  misspent &
  (piddling pity)
  unspent
has poured itself off into
a big jar, jug, cistern, pool,
bog, mere, lake, bay, or
ocean of grief but
  this was a morning, like
  any other, for anything,

a whistling colleague,
an assignation finally
accomplished, a birth,
death, a pheasant screeching

achieve an identity,
find a direction, such achieving
leaves behind as much as it finds

choose short-term goals and having
realized them, wait for the grave
wandering afloat the landscape
to find you

have long-range, even impossible,
goals and
you will complete no work
but you will,
eyes on the sky, stumble astonished
into the grave,
your work left
to others, an inheritance

imbalance providing the
illusion of direction,
the loops, sways
of exaggeration, we can, ah,
and, therefore

could a shady
spot of the peace
everlasting patch
the wretched ways
and byways of the
lusty & hard-to-take!

oh, but we should not rail!
everything but our understanding
is flawless

the hemlocks are
sensitive wind instruments
    you can
    judge by the thicket
    that it's calm
but just then the tips of
hemlock branches pick
up the frailest motions,
    the long branches, you
    know, rise out in high
    bow-boughs from the trunk
    and secondary branches
    branch off,
a dense replication and
registration so that
when the wind blows branch
tip and branch tip
try out the sways and lofts
of space and
    sure enough
    here and there
branch tips intermingle
and where they often
intermingle (summarizing
prevailingness)
the tips lose needles,
fray,
and, no way proved to go,
the tip dies
and growth takes place at
another tip:
each way won or free:

a little past four
it has turned so clear
the sky bright blue
    cold
    the blacktipped brown

caterpillars
lured out
by yesterday's heat
circle crinkled in the grass
now (one on the garage floor)
the teens cold working on
them: spring steps up
warmly saying
bud bloom sprout shoot
and arctic highs
mow the answering down:
to endure
a thing must speak
more slowly than
highs & lows

You Can

You can
walking with the wind
think yourself
becalmed
but turning to return
find yourself
in a ten-mile-an-hour gale
    and on a great
    bright
    cold morning like
this that
calm thirty degrees
drops
chilling windchill degrees:
but the birds
are a chorus,
the jay's big vocabulary:
the sparrow
is hauling straw
up to a streetlight
(nitelite)
sheets of ice standing in
v-bottomed ditches
and a vapor-ice
of white haze
on grass near water:
    grackle, crow, cardinal,
    robin, birds but no bees:
according to the weather forecast
here comes another warm
spell up to the sixties:
lately the temperature
has been up & down on
a four-day cycle,

teens to seventies,
really rolling differentials,
spiraling through dragging
nordic or tropic skirts:
let's not get into that:
cunt is disturbing

today if it goes to 45
caterpillars run down outside
may nick away in the sun
 the lilyshoots
 though
 or also,
  deeply puzzled,
  rush out firm
  to sixty degrees
  but bend stain-limp
  to the teens
scare crows
raise money
field mice

they said I ought to get
a stereo because
when from seventy you subtract
fifty it only leaves
you twenty mo'
for stereo
(lessen yall gits lucky)
you do do do, too

  The Wife's Plaint

There may be
more room on
the outside than
on the inside but
there's more

room on the
outside outside than
on the
outside inside.

    may hernias
rot in your
soup! the disgusting
husband said:

may
cocksuckers ululate on
your doorstep! the
precious wife replied:

may the worms
in your round worms
need worming & may
a great Swish
swallow your Knob!

french-freud

Cunit

Cunit

    close as i can
    come without being there

cuneus is okay and cunette
fellow said he got his
tongue hung
in one
once (which I never believed)
and said whenever he did
the rest of it
started in to pecking on him
is what he said
till he couldn't tell
whether he was coming or
going
and his whole tongue got
covered with red-peckered
welts like you never seen
cunnythumber
slurp slop
I never met a man
with a dirty mouth
(delicacy governs true passions)
that had any real
respect or deserved any

everybody well-adjusted
to sex keeps his mouth shut

the elm is darkening
with mere
budbead

I saw this morning
come out on the porch steps
and on a leaf of periwinkle
a beadblack bug
hemispheric so as
nearly to stick flat
to leaf or slate
two red eyes
one on either wing

It's a Wonder the Body

It's a wonder the body
goes on making
things not thought
well of, saliva, for example,

wondrous devising
containing
water, mucin, protein, salts,
and a starch-splitting
enzyme
   that has been accorded little
common knowledge and small
applause, like great servants
who flawlessly
disappear
into their work

eyes spread around
inside scraps,
tips, filaments of
brand new or newly
worn attraction

aphids that eat up the
roses are
as pretty
as roses
   twice as green,
    their dew honey,
    and their petals fly

the bigeye belly
is
love's Polyphemos

maggots like
undertakers (too)
work dead stuff
but are unlike
livelier

a gray warm
day with sprinkles
not met on concrete

I just went for a walk by the brook
(high brooks are interesting,
the collections aimless
above the slope drop)
geese again

Today Was Like Vomiting

Today was like vomiting:
all morning and until
midafternoon
the wind scoured the trees
like the dry heaves
blustering dust and pollen
till finally it brought
the clouds up
and by four the smallest
rain came with a quieting
wind and then later the
true tensions found themselves
and wind and cloud
delivered the shaking
spouting flood we'd been
waiting for
    now there will
    be some ease
    the birds can settle
    we can have dusk,
dinner's smooth time

because winter cut a deeper
trench this year than usual
  I feared last year's
  mockingbird might not make
  it back or through
but there
down in my neighbor's
orchardlike yard
  I saw the bird dive
  spread those barred
  rounded-off wings
  and splash into trilling song:

I saw that yesterday:
you know how a robin can get
variable in a pellucid dusk
and sound remarkable
    but not quite make it, as
    the mockingbird
    can hold no vocal candlestick
    to the woodlark
sound's most beautiful song

    Showers

    The grass is
    green by
    the time the
    clouds are blue

how much
more blowing
will establish
spring

It's April 1

It's April 1
the willow's yellow's
  misting green:
adding white maybe
tonight or tomorrow

Canadian air 30 below above
the clouds has
settled into the midlands
and is moving eastward
  this will bring
  ground temperatures
  within range
  of the structural
  flare-out snow

    (o (o   a look-see
    (o o)   slightly more direct
    (- (-   shut-eye
    ($ ($ American dream
    (* (*   34" bust

great logs
dragged to the fireplace are
with ashspoon dipped away

earthworms are only
little long people

I'm Unwilling

I'm unwilling
to write this
morning but
      things
keep nudging me
to sidle with
them into
words,
    what is it, even a tension
    in the mind
wants to play
itself
through the lit stage
wing to wing,
across and through
severe illumination,
burning every crick
and hue
of the hidden out;
to be announced!
pronounced!
shaped, made, attended
to, to have occurred as
an item of what was,
to be a thing that is

the bloom shed of the
maple is
spring's
first fall   the maple itself
          a falls
          the milling fall making
          of bloom parts
          to hold through winter
          and open

                    to spring's first warmth
                    and fall
(so early this year!
midFeb)

the syrup keeps
rising through the trunk,
wooden fountain,
and always from
the replications and
rondures, slope heights,
of the tree
spill
the bloom parts
the sent
wide reaches of pollen, the
lightgathering, dismissed
leaves, hunting, spinning
seed
                    the tree,
                    holding to one place,
                    moves as far
                    as possible
                    abroad, away, away
                    to other holdings

it is not for the poet to
speak the speakable
that which long known & said
requires no energy
of finding or forming but to
murmur, stammer, swear, and
sing on the edges of or around
or deep into the unspeakable—
the unspeakable, silent sorrow!
the unspeakable, silent joy!

there was a time in January
when the light was barren

moving in blurs and glows
between clouds and falling
on the snow-and-ice-enameled
hills, the streaks and
thickets
of ice-brush
   like ink brushwork
   ornamentation:
the ridge, I thought,
moves, flows, and
I was held by a power
beyond all but silence
to contain

a joy inexpressible,
inexcusable

standing not away or at an
opposite pole but
in the midst of which
grief
like high icy ghosts of
lombardies
slow-swayed!

      things arranged
      at their centers so
      that when we
      grasp them
      they turn slightly
      (like a dishwasher
      dial) and go into
      another tone or slant
      or cycle or flatly
      from kind to kind

quandary lies centrally in balancing wings
so much so that as we draw near, the directness of

our sight blinds us to the full facetal radiality
so we are not likely ever to dissolve the knot because
we work against ourselves when we hope to for if
we did, behold, the world and we would stop: how
grateful we must be that as we reach to take the
much desired in hand it loses shape and color and
drifts apart and must be looked for all over again
    so are we shoveled
    forward half unwillingly
    into the future (where futurity is lost)

praise or railing—
these two the sky equally
takes up unlimited
and lets vanish

The Sky Clabbered Up with

The sky clabbered up with
blue-clabber clouds
and
   (meanwhile the temperature
   falling off)
the whey-gray whey rose
shutting off from earthly
view the fine white
cumulus heights (yogurt)
   but still whereas and
   whenever he did
the cold kept coming and
pretty soon drops
of rain
lost sharp swift
substance
   and blurred their way
   down white
   (white down)
   big clumpy snow mixed with
   rain, one thing popcorn
   and the other popcorn popped

there's no accumulation
anywhere
on hemlock, garage, lily
shoot, yew, nor in crocus
cup, nor forsythia bell
   whenever it did & any
   flake touches anything
   it crumbles, shrinks,
   a little bit
   of nearly nothing

A Single Fact

A single fact
inadmissible into
sound generates
billows of volubility
whereas said out
it would turn
small as
a drop of rain   I looked down the
                   brook at the outblanking
                   high glaze
                   running water gets when light
                   falls (into) against it
                   and thought how polished
                   water lofts ripples stone still
                   almost

and about how the dullish gold
gets down between the
radiant-gray ledge shoulders
and holds color over each brook-step
ledge to ledge down the hill
      until of course (!)
      everything narrows
      and disappears going down
into the burial of itself
slope-lowering
burial from my sight though
for others beneath me
it makes sights and tunes

It Does Not Rain in

It does not rain in
air-conditioned rooms
and the fan-wind blows
(dust weaves in the rooms
looms and glooms
of loom-gloom) leaves
pittering across
dome-locked, skyless pavilions
are grocery tickets or nasal
tissues

    (the brown
    bushbrush
    here
    though hazes greenly
    dense)

snot rags

I feel like a master:
nothing happens here that I
do not wish and
everything responds

    (when we arrive at the
    center
    a wing-gate flies open
    and turns
    us into new material
    out)

like water in
eddy
about to find

restful rondure
then sliced
from its widest
circumference
downstream

cold
currents settle
from polar ice
bottomward
like falls

motion holding moving—
(the ripple I spoke of the
other day,
now the eddy,
but also the millennial
deep bends &
sweeps of rock forms
and sea currents)

there's ice under ice in
Anarctica so old
it's lost to count
but is still pressing down:
 the earth, mantle-deep or
 crust adjustment,
 is responding to that:

I see into so much every day
(sd the obstetrician)
my breakfast nooky quivers

mostly cloudy at sunrise but
now turning clear blue in
spots and a turning up and down
of light (we may go to
McDonald's for lunch!)

One Loves

One loves
absolutely and
forever
   anything else is
something else

in wax museums
men have
wax balls
but in fire
museums
balls of fire

I know only one
thing to talk
about (poetry)
and that
covers everything

(even on a moist morning
midMarch, the street
showered still-wet,
flocks of birds foliating,
defoliating shrubs and
trees, the cardinal singly
chirping, even on such a
morning, the word, pliant,
suppliant,
wrenching shinnies up the
ash-damp heights
and higher cries out in the
cindery desert for an
answerer)

      headstone-shade snow
      melts slowly

it still can't quite clear off
or get cloudy—
dwelling mixed
in between
some of both and not much of either

The Miltonic (Miltownic) Isn't

The miltonic (miltownic) isn't
milty or come
to think of it   all you can do
tonic   with a day like today is
either   slice it and eat
     it, cake
     blue, radiant,
     frill green, also
the maple   just-right cool
bloomparts, cast millings,
have shrunk into meal, so
dry, granola, forsooth,
that stepped on they turn
snuff-dusty, a
prepared, engineered reentry:

I do not wish to speak too
highly of nature where only
what can work works,
only the possible possible
(though I like brooks
better than diamonds)
     (no wonder things work in and
     out so well together because
     if they didn't they wouldn't
work long)
(the mind wishes to design other works)

that so much should come
to nothing, an abundance!
so much design be dust!
at-onceness
startles marveling

my head, the
skull grown
brittle thin,
I hold it
in my hand:
it is the world
to me: I
turn it some
as if
it were a
precious object:
but it is
mainly hollow
without longitude
or latitude,
good for lolling
and wobbling
when I
open a book
to a strict or
famous verse

My Father Used to Tell of an

My father used to tell of an
old lady so old
they ran her down and knocked
her in the head with
a lightered knot
to bury her (then
there was another
one so old
she dried up and turned
to something good to eat)

what my father enjoyed
most—in terms of pure,
high pleasure—was
scaring things: I remember
one day he and
I were coming up in Aunt
Lottie's yard
when there were these
ducks ambling
along in the morning sun,
a few drakes, hens, and a string of
ducklings,
and my father took off his
strawhat and
shot it spinning out sailing in
a fast curving glide over the
ducks so they
thought they were being
swooped by a hawk,
and they just, it looked
like, hunkered down on their
rearends and slid all the
way like they were

greased right under the house
   (in those days houses
   were built up off the ground)
my father laughed the purest,
highest laughter
till he bent over
thinking about those
ducks sliding under
there over nothing

my father, if you could rise
up to where he was at, knew
how to get fun straight
out of things
    he was a legend
    in my lifetime

I remember when he was so
strong he could carry me and
my sister, one leaning to
each shoulder, with our
feet in the big wooden slop bucket:
he died with not a leg
to stand on

yesterday afternoon it snowed &
I scribbled: "more
uncertain (showery) glory,
flurries and sunshine, the
ground dry because as the
flakes melt on touch the sun
gives the moisture back to
the wind, also uncertain, the
flakes steeply or widely
rising almost as much as
falling but so thin-scattered,
so fine hardly
more than an uninformed

bluster—really nice, the
sun cracking stark bright off
one cloudhead and plunging
paling and dissolving like a
flake into a new blue summit"

today's spanking bright blue
(gold willows and green evergreens)
and chilly, a
little fresh-windy, great day for a walk

Arm's Length Renders One

Arm's length renders one
helpless
   (stiff and loud)
where one cannot intimately
and warmly tickle tits
or drive to bust
balls
      one must seek
      out the subtleties
      and rapid
adjustments, suggestions, and
speed of the middle way,
using the extreme only as a
total realization of
potential (punch in face):
        spring drought,
no significant
precipitation for ten days at
least, has persuaded the
brook down to a wink here
and there (lust or
rebellion) and
the ground has cracked as if
to swallow birds or fire,
not seed: it's warming up
this morning, to 40, but
forecast for tomorrow is
cold, blusters, and snow flurries:

the poem hangs
on like winter,
words flying out and dropping
to greet
the leftover flurries and

chills:
night before last was 19 but
nothing was killed, just hit
scorched with the blahs:
  one Sunday when I was
  eleven my father and
  I found the "mineral"
  spring back
  below the Hinson Field in
  the woods
  and we sat down where
  the little hill fell away
  toward the swamp and talked:
  I carved my father's
  initials and my own in
  a treetrunk and 1937:
I would not want to see that
work again

I'm the Type

I'm the type
  FARM BOY MAKES GOOD
    (not farming)

or, with more development tho
still very commonly,
Redneck Kid Grows Up On
Farm Goes Through Depression
But Thanks To Being In
Big War Goes To College
Gets Big Job Making
Big Money
    (relatively speaking)

so that I am not much of a
person after all and
do not need be, the
lineations of the type
include egregious individuality

broaden lineation or
replicate included space

      because of last fall's
      late bloom-thinning
      the forsythia is
      this year not a
      golden bulwark but a
      yellow sprinkle bush

when the wind blows through
my round yew
it changes direction so many
times to get round the branches

and needle leaves
it wears itself out
half way through:
eventually, though, demolished
smooth, really put together,
it floats on through and out,
a massive, indifferent
tranquility available to give
substance to quick turns or
swerves

REDNECK FARM BOY WRITE GOOD
(doesn't sell much)
WRITE VERY GOOD
(but misses
farm, etc., also other rednecks)
MAKE NO MONEY
BUT
WRITE NICE
(tries hard)
(misses the mules and cows,
hogs and chickens, misses
the rain making little
rivers, well-figured with
tributaries, through the
sand yard)

REDNECK UNDERSTAND OTHERS
WRITE A LOT
(books too good
to sell, leave on
shelf in bookstore)

REDNECK START TO SOUND LIKE
INDIAN

him remember Indian burial
mounds in woods, sandy pine woods,

also used to plow up arrowheads
and not think much of it

HIM REDNECK
OPERATE UNDER TOTEM
WASP
(barefoot all summer)
(get hookworm)
(pale neck)

Snow Showed a Full Range

Snow showed a full range
today, showers at six
this morning with
the temperature falling
through sleet and grainy,
gritty, and, now, dusty
snow
    a tying-off action with
cold striking, congealing, the
last skirts of action

the lawn is whiter than green
the hemlocks hold touchy sprays

No Matter

No matter
　how
　　driving
　　　fast or
　　　dense
　　　　(to speak of
whited air, indeed, the lake
was wiped out, and the
opposite ridge's
fields,
house-clusters, dairy barns
and silos
fell under) the flakes all
afternoon,
the ground would take no
steady impression
and the highway not stay wet:
　　big icicles hung off the
　　car like the brocade and
　　strings of epaulets but
the temperature held just
where an outflash of sun
would thaw them loose
so the sun and clouds
needled sewing and unsewing
the white sheets
dyeing and bleaching

so it snowed and snowed
the wind blew and the
flakes flew
and it added up to a
passing

the lily shoots
hold scoops and sloops of
snow
(keeps off the grass)

and the hairy hollyhock's
young leaves and the hairy
green tongues of oriental poppy
had the right way to
hold snow so it would last
fluffed up on stiff hairs
(hairy tongues)

I hope winter will not
end like a Beethoven symphony
with big bams and
flurries into June but that
it will ease off
like something by Debussy
so you hardly miss it

It's So Dry the Brook, down

It's so dry the brook, down
to nearly nothing to do
falls as if asleep, coasting,
between ledge spills

(some old men walk sloped
forward in a stumble-run,
the regular, keyed rhythm
surpassed
into a soothing high dance)

spray churned from the
commotion of a slight ledge
spill, though, can sprinkle
overhanging branches
so they freeze loaded in cold
weather, big ice nodes and
chunks interweaving branches so
as to ride in hard
high separation
from the central rush,
melt lasting from one cold spell
to the next

there is by the gorge
a slope so steep
no one interferes with its
brush and trees
(unshaken by height chills)
nature is not a
palimpsest there but a clear book

vine
limber enough to move

entangles a high branch
which, snapping off,
sways, held, in the
great tree's
windy shoals

that which rising
takes over can break
down and, no longer
to be let go, no longer uphold

nature's message is, for
the special reader,
though clear, sometimes written
as on a tablet underwater,
the message will blur and
seem to run but
declare itself in a smooth
moment to great attention

Today Will Beat Anything

Today will beat anything:
a full day of clarity
up to seventy: but
still no rain
(bright skies starving skies)
and the last precipitation
which was snow, though it
fell blanking out the
world, all but the very
immediate, had no effect on
the ground, a dampening that
did not close up the
cracks, riffles of snow on
the lawn quickly evaporating:
I declare I started to get
out the hose and commence
to water, because that
fertilizer I had the young
man sprinkle about
the hedges and under the trees
has been lying out there feed-dry
for two weeks:
     when you consider how
     dry it is
it's amazing the brook still
runs, clips, brook-brisk: the
ground must be holding
at a height plenty:

it is so odd, upon waking
from a nap, to think that
one's body, including the
back of one's hand, one's
fingernails, the calves

and ankles, the face, these
things one's own, are also
implicated and will die,
too, with one, each
its going away

    oneself I sing,
    a person apart,
    shoved aside,
    silenced

cross references

seems the bushes are being
sprayed from a distance green

will the universe become
forever dark:
    once in a lifetime

Sight Can Go Quickly, Aerial, Where

Sight can go quickly, aerial, where
feet can go not at all

scale clouds out of
prison windows,
splash from heights into lakes
(not drowning, not even
getting wet)

from high boughs can
spot rescue in the hills
though marshlands intervene

oh, sight! sight!
how light you make us
and how heavy!

      say now
      pay later

spring drought's good for being
bad for molds
and fluffy funguses that leap
snarl-red in dampness or gross blue:
good for giving the roots
of young sprouts occasion to
lengthen into the soil and
be ready for rain when it
comes: good probably
for slowing and toughening
growth so it can better
resist frost
sure to be be back: good
for killing off anything

too much or too weak: good
for getting early pollen
up into the atmosphere:

if butterflies wrote letters
of recommendation their wings
would crack: ripples on brooks
don't advise or recommend
other ripples, and shale spills
to and finds alignment with
brook flow

supposed to go to 80
today, probably did:
the early tulips, three
scarlet-velvet red, opened
this morning just in
time to be rained in by
a trivial shower: all
that negligible
clouding up and passing over!

These Days Most

These days most
any brown stick
sprouts a green tip

      how could you, walking in the mts,
      be as big as the mts: only by
      wandering: aimlessness
      is as big as mts

The Cardinal, Slanted Watershed

The cardinal, slanted watershed,
in sprouting treebranch
singly singing

and some small bird, grayish
with yellowish back feathers,
dipples and dabbles in the
hemlock boughs, flies almost
hard-still into the willowy
withery boughs and hangs
softly on:
the delicate greenworm haunts
terminal tips

unseasonably this
unseasonably that   my
                        tendency
                to exaggerate
                has
        vastly diminished

why, a lady along the way
inquires, is your motor running
so fast:
and I say, is there nothing
to catch or flee:
she says, you're too slow now,
anyway, aren't you, to catch anything
fine: and whatever has not
already overtaken you is
not coming:

madam, I say, I am not
frail and

the weather may improve: she says,
you know those sunny rooms,
enclosed porches, that lie
off the sides of kitchens,
those long rooms with
lounge chairs and hanging green
blades and tongues of
cactus and big-eared begonias:
that is what you have caught,
has caught up with you: come
in: the afternoon sweeps
through here on a good day:

madam, I say, the long
boxes of empty afternoons, I
had anticipated fierier affairs:

come, she said: you
thought you saw something:
it was nothing:

I, he said, going in, am
barely able to conceive . . . or
concede belief

One Desires the Cutting

One desires the cutting
glassy edges of
nearly-wordless poems

but one yearns
for the openness of context,
too, so as to tell

what urn or bottle broke:
restore nothing:
we want nothing back:

contexts (enclosures) show
what ruin we're wrecking in
or passing by,
passers-by or guides

the flawless evidence favoring
death leaves us
unconvinced
and we're ready
on no evidence
to believe we live forever

flasher   laser   lasher
slasher   maser   masher

in long views
even great traditions
are often bulges
from a main line

I Wonder If Pagan Is

I wonder if *pagan* is
unfairly defined in the dictionary,
a shade too much lean to bacchic
as if it were not serious or moral, or
as manifested by early man,
nature-boy innocence, not true:
look it up:

suspicions confirmed!
oh, well, it takes a while
to turn or bust up
a current
(without affecting the climate)
here is room
in this long poem's thickets and byways,
flyby's, big timber, high marsh, and
sea lane, for one to turn the wrong way
around this hedge, streamfork
or that, boulder,
pavilion ledge
and take on
unnoticed a different coloring
as if one had come
surprisingly suddenly from
a pure place or belief:
if you cannot choose,
here I will lose (hide) you,
wind and unwind you till you
will be a found astonishment: you
will be sitting on a stump
by a brook and a beautiful woman will
come by and say, who are you,
and you will say, I am a new man:
(then you will have completed

pilgrimage, and begun):
let us not patch up anything:
let us have it or tear it out:

   one or two will get lost
   perhaps in a ravine and
   forget it is not Eden:
   they will concentrate
   one on the other: nature
   will align its major
   forces through them and every
   morning shove itself into
   their mouths, a fresh
   apple!
my outrage, my anger is
oceanic: it is free as
my verse: lovingly I empty
myself of it: lovingly I write
out my loathing:
I would sell my book to
millions to find one to love

   slender willowy
   in a waterfall

Rage Spells More of My Words Right

Rage spells more of my words right
than any other feeling

the big red sun just set
under two vapor trails that
diverge from a crossing in
the sky, the planes so high
they can't be heard—but
I have found, I think, a
copy of the northern hermit
thrush and I've been trying
to read it—a frailer, less
fluid, less crystalline-breaking sound
than the southern woodlark
but still plaintive,
liquid bell-clarity, glade music:

my crazy rage, depression,
my insulted silence, along
with all my dissolving talk,
my playing tensions out while
others twist believable
tensions tight:
all nothing! when it goes it
leaves
behind inexpressible beauty!
the happiness of lingo

On This Day Noteworthily Warm

On this day noteworthily warm
fossil fuel is 3¢ a ton or vat

the tough sweet element in
man . . . the newsman, no matter
how he feels, comes up
with news, the weatherman
with weather, the
bread&milk man doesn't come anymore

the forecaster for today
forecasts
einen thunderstormen may
blusterbufferoomen through:

gossamer-in-the-wind glint,
(three sheets)
trees-in-the-breeze sneeze,
spruce worms, little greenies,
dangling, squirming

say it was 93 downtown
yesterday: about as hot
today: but I think
there's cooling
in the evening breeze

Some Nights I Go Out to Piss

Some nights I go out to piss
among the big black scary shrubs:
the tinkling stars
don't seem to mind:

cruddy crude   stars & stones
  ruddy   rude   silent & naked

odd that where no one is to have
anything, not even his
own life,
    having is the game:
that where no one is to win
but indeed lose losing
   itself
   the game is winning:
and where not a single love,
mother-child, lover-girl, man-son,
is to hold,
   love settles in:
odd, odd that as the days go
by so rich, so lost, one fool, trying to save it,
wastes the day

contradiction is a center
turning around makes
another place to go

nasty century! whose
enlightenment
fills the air with smoke,
darkens the day

My Structure Is, Like the

My structure is, like the
bug's, external:
rubbing up against others, I
acquire form: mingling
my speech with that of others,
I annex scaffolding:
like a man in a well, I kick
one wall, brace my back
against the other, to work my way up:
inside, I am too soft to point
a piling, my hard walls
wet sheets on a line:
    Phyllis and John
    have gone off
    for a few days,
    which they need, I suspect,
    and I am,
    alas, alone:
(terror, my pet lion)
the catkins
(small lions)
hard-sharp have
lengthened fluffy-long and waggly:

it's better to be tough
and free than
to bawl and chain

    I notice on my
    walks that when
    I move everything
    moves!—
    so much seeming
    to the one motion!

pollen burn

had a voice and
couldn't place it

my neighbor's dog (big shaggy
black&white) died late last
fall in cold's fringe
and was buried in a
small clearing in the hedge:
this spring
I've expected the ground
to spew, corruption
work up,
but the mound has given
notice neither outward nor inward:

there's a slope-lawn down by
the brook whereon a young
birch frilly in early-girlish
leaf seems to have been caught
raining, catkins icicle long and thick:
girlish or boyish, in case one
is one and the other, other:
up the street a bit, a man
has set out two birch, one
three-trunked and the other four-

sometimes I twist out a roll
of nearly-dry white snot and it
unwinds some in my fingers
so disgusting

star stump stone stare stub stem stob
post oak
white oak
ghost oak
            so much works flawed

it makes you think
perfection not one of
nature's hangups: the
crow gets by with a feather-gap
or so in his wing,
the robin is full of worms, and
I have teeth missing trailertrucks
ride through: still, nature
doesn't lose count: it puts
away
everything it brings to life—
to perfection:

You Think of the Sun That It

You think of the sun that it
burns to burn
and that the soul for its own
brightness burns

but the sun burns right to
the brim of necessity,
its floes dipping and
plunging to averaged effect,
sun spots, flares, in-feed
of interstellar trash, outflow of
radiance through whatever
cloth of radiance, an
historical burn, one-way,
out with surrounding
accidence wide open, stray
chunk pulled in, suns
driving to meet at a fast
sharp point, so many necessities,
so many sides
that the sun cannot burn for
a reason for any reason but
to burn
as the soul burns
to show and shed its brightness

being is the summary
of incalculable interpenetrant
necessity

        motion
        itself is the fine
tuning by which the earth
flies neither into space

nor the sun:
however
fine and open the adjustments
though
the structures of motion
exceed all strength of steel
woven, stainlessly wound:

          rock whereon much
          is founded will
          split but motion
          is
polished by millions of years
(the foundation
in nothingness, deeply
based, towers highest)

I thought, to water the bees,
hornets, wasps, &c., I would
put a bucket under the faucet
outside that leaks so little:
but I thought if I set it flat
I will have a full bucket,
the brim brimming wet all
around: so I thought I must
slant the bucket (but not
enough to exclude the drop) and
leave a part of the
brim-arc dry so the things can
light: but what, I thought,
will hold a bucket at 45 degrees:
everything hassles me: the truth
is I do not know
how to water wasps: a good
try, though, would be the
slightest slant, a mere lean,
to dry off a crescent, a
fine moon; then,

the things could land on the
high rim and walk as deep as
need be into the refreshing
flood: intricacy has as many
in's as out's:
(the good part about leaning
the bucket is that if the bee
fell in he would gradually
mosey over to the lip-spill
where his legs would catch
rimbottom: then he could loft
and shake his wings and
tiptoe to safety)

if people who can think of
nothing to do would
water bees
they would find themselves
working with the principles
of the universe, a mind-blowing
and consciousness-raising
experience, I suspect)
      ♪♪♪
short-winged swallows
      ♯
using round nails
      ♭ ♭♭♭♭♭ ♭
turkish birds
      ♯♯♯♯♯♯♯
enslaved turkish birds
      ❀❀❀❀❀❀
ain't that purty
      ᑫᑫ
longing for deconstruction
      ☻☻
some other time
      ᑫᑫ
frameworked

if I could write a poem a
thousand pages long my point
would be established: every line
delightful but all you wd have
to do is lift it to discover
its weight and irrelevance!

unevenness had begun to
establish itself in my lawn
when I got out the mower
and, for the small, let
a lot of room in from the top
(so much for income tax)

sweet clarity
reconciled at
great depth
                    regular rational
discourse is good for
taking care
of highways, pick up the trash,
trim the hedges, oil the
cracks, while the imagination
works on giving birth to some
other form of travel

am I law and outlaw, pope and
pensioner, sage and fool,
writer and reader, male and
female, am I, sir, a small
town (in microcosm) where
this one and that one is
sometimes mayor, where at
any rate, government
concerns all:

it's five o'clock, brightly
cold and somedeal chilly: I
have just awakened, having,
after cutting the grass and
getting sweaty, fallen
asleep, sweat-chilled, in the
big chair: I am hungry: I
do not know whether I will go
downstairs and scramble a
couple of eggs, then have a
bite at Neil's later (where
I'm invited to be with Harold
and others at 7:30 but where,
since I was too nervous to
attend the afternoon sessions
of lectures, I may not go) or
go to MacDonald's for a Big
Mac (I think I'll do that)
and have a bite later at Neil's
or not have anything till I
get to Neil's—most unlikely

I already came home at 2:30
and fed my city a fresh
banana dunked milky in frosty
flakes: I should not be
hungry: but it is cold and
I cut the grass: and Phyllis
and John are not here, and I
feel the need of something it
is so bright:

I do not care what anybody
thinks of anything, really:
that is to say, I have not
found the flavor of orange
juice diminished or increased

by this or that approach to
Heidegger or Harmonium: I
believe the constituency of
water has remained constant
since the Pleides:
I don't think that any
attitude I take to spider webs
will faze flies: have you seen
Stanley Fish in the flesh:
words sweep around but then
just miss to form their own
world: think what a
caterpillar thinks: he holds
the universe between his
horny toes and eats it in
worky swatches!

    sublemonade
    sublimeade

not only can we not look into
the sun but it sweeping out
its light as if eliminates
what it illuminates: that
the center of light
should be blind! well, I
must go off hamburgerward:
           (delicious)
on full alert
  massive layoffs
    hurt his chances (a strong
case for continuing its
existence)
    positive developments
(receptive to such a move)
normalize relations
totally fallacious allegation (lie)

death secures us from
death, words slug for our redemption
always a swing and a miss, meanwhile
it's balls & bacon as usual, conception
and decay, laughter and tears,
the explosive, incredible mix

Snow

Snow   wons
            mons

since we must die,
sweet completeness will
not have us wait in attendance
on our bodies
while workers fatten
and disperse and find
slick tunnels to
flight and the rich (or poor)
man's table,
while roots explore the
forehead and settle in the
ears, while the burrowing
beetle swims through or
around the eye (like a planet)
while the water rises and
the body log
spins, the bottom-gazing
face: how, I mean,
nice that though we know this
we need not witness the
knowing of this

life, that can be death
enough, *that* we need
and know, so that as we
enter into death we slip
out of it
like wrapping off the
chocolate:

wooden boxes eventually "give,"

the rain finds a hole and bores
through, milling the bones and mound
gravel: on such a day of happenings,
those who love go here and there

four days of clouds, two days
of rain, the temperature
steadily falling, this morning
before dawn the rain ran into
deep temperatures that popped
it white and the spruce,
cedar, grass, roofs, and all
tolerable surfaces took on
the accumulation of white and
when everybody got up today
he had something to talk
about: from 93 to 30:
some of the snow lingers in
the cedar hedges almost at
the freezing mark: it has
changed from white to look
almost like water but there is
still ice enough to hold
it in the boughs, so it cannot
fall, held water, islands of
snow:

then there is the presence in
the head, a figure that never
speaks, immortal, apparently,
who, even in one's death, has
nothing to do with what is
taking place and will not credit
its reality, too bemused for
assent or concern

grit, flakes, sleet, fluff
all day the snow snowed in

vain
nothing but green in the
grass nothing but leaves
in the trees

It Snowed All Night Snow

It snowed all night snow
like pear-petal snow and has
snowed all
morning, skimpy flakes,
solitary, wandering schools:

the clouds, just discernibly
clouds from the general gray,
move on in a brisk
wind: the buttercups,
leant over, have surrendered
their sturdy forms to limp
wastrelness: the birds have
vanished into bushes:

what has come over you

if a rope were tied between
two posts
there would be most play in
the middle: coming out
of the middle, the play
diminishing, one faces
the attached fact, the hard
narrowing and shortening,
the play gone out:

who who had
anything else
to be interested
in would be
interested in
the weather

we mill in a room where
a conveyor belt now and
then entangles and brings down
one who, mindlessly, is carried out:
the others mill
and scramble, touching bottom
lightly, getting high
on the archy:
verse the room's ventilator

light showers soak my shoes
verse writers croak my nerves

   hard feelings

you know when
something is wrong
how grateful you
have not been

how many
shocks of enlightenment
burn out
a tradition!

after I have been
myself enough I will
die and go
on being universe

modren friend when dil thou do
reaching from end to end
cripes that my bed were in my arms
and I in my love again

Drip Drip

Drip drip
truck it

in our galaxy alone
(billions of others)
extraterrestrial
noncelestial life

S P A C E

the reality man has lately
tried to conceive
in which, however,
solid ground,
scaffolding

ten billion people
may dance on the
pinhead of the earth's
center

undercut

footings, literally, what is
our footing,
not rock, motion, space—
nothingness!
              (and the realization,
              tho hard,
              that that
is the strongest
footing, providing most
options, the greatest
range of possibility) how

fortunate that we
did not have it
the way we thought we
wanted it:

the primate touching
down lightly on
the ground
now, three million years later,
ready to give up the ground

THE GROUND ERA

THE SPACE ERA

the heavens acquire another
side, a landing

both feet on the ground
no feet on the ground

there is an animal, louse-like,
but smaller, antennaed, grazing
the winter month of dust on
the bathroom windowsill:

I love a plant
I think too much
I bought it
I placed it by my bed
I think
I love it too much

a ray of sunlight just (11:44 a.m.)
broke through and hit
across the leaves of
my plant whose hunger and
pleasure I feel I think

some sit home and think
about their feelings but
others land elsewhere

the land grows peripheral
and less secure
and secure nothingness moves
centerward

my plant!
what is it sitting on,
the center of the galaxy,
a composition of centers
of galaxies!
the bedsidetable:

    drip drip
    the sky is drying
    hot snow

the sky like water
standing in a rowed field!
the furrows of cloud pull
apart and show
the sky filling the ruts
blue and clear

mucous   it cannot snoo
vomit   at forty too
gush

Some Fluffy, Long-Swaggly Catkins

Some fluffy, long-swaggly catkins
have fallen to the ground, heads
swung round in looped resentment
or resignation, fashionable cousins
to the earthworm:
    the brook has moved into
higher flow, sustained by last night's
slow-soaker: this morning
the sky's rinsed
blue, the hazy blue of color informing
itself, interrupted here and there
by ranges of white mountains:

      if, as appears likely,
      reality is not a wit solid
      but a dream another
      head, perhaps, is dreaming,
        why, then . . .

what difference does
what we think and say make:
have the mountains responded:
is there word from
the sea: has the sky
looped down to question us:

broadcast gathers coincidence:

        people have
        scoffed, perhaps,
        because from my
upland upstate shelter I've
looked out on the universe:
but in time it will appear

mean to have looked out on less:
   the grave quits
   speculation:
   feel the astonishment
   of buried roominess!
   a twinkledom in the deep!

    roots
    would coil
    and nest
    in the eye
    sockets

        why but
        clapper-like
        the hard point
        of the catkin
        unopened sways
        a tip of weight
        so the fuzzy
        mechanisms and
        gold pavilions
        of dispersal can
        catch and tangle
        with the wind,
        the ocean whose
        currents find
        otherness

I think I am sick with a pure
interest in beauty,
a joy skinny as a fountain
that erupts
through entanglements
for real loft before gravity
unfurls fall's umbrella

the wind's rinse over ice-enameled
hill-ridges! how beautiful

all winter, the light flowing
and riding, the dark sharp
lines of hedgerow! too
spare, so lean!

after sunrise this morning the sky
cleared and the sun
hit the windows with light,
the indoor plants standing as if
in celebration:
and all day has been
beautiful, the redbud blooming,
apple trees blossoming, so
many scents and colors, the
brown fingers of spruce
shaking dust, so much and
water trickling in the
ditches, trickling
disconcerted like ridge water

I break poetry off
I have not earned very much
I am not worthy of the
energy that winds up
spruce tops and floats off
into the air still winding,
also I am denied much,
this beauty, though very
beautiful, is an inconsiderable
feast,
a snack enlarged to
astonishment where love
has little meeting

My Father, I Hollow for You

My father, I hollow for you
   in the ditches
O my father, I say,
and when brook light, mirrored,
worms
   against the stone ledges
   I think it an unveiling
or coming loose, unsheathing
of flies
O apparition, I cry,
   you have entered in
   and how may you come
   out again
   your teeth will not
   root
   your eyes cannot
unwrinkle, your handbones
may not quiver and stir
O, my father, I cry,
are you returning:
I breathe and see:
it is not you yet it is you

I Knew

I knew
if I

went for
a walk

I'd get
my feet

wet but
only so

I Cannot Re-wind the Brook

I cannot re-wind the brook,
back it up and make
it flow through again ten
times till
it achieves the highest
compression, the concentrated
essential, of being a brook,
brookness finally found and
held away from all brooks:

but the brook shoots muddy
with perfect
accuracy the morning after
rain and in
a dry season
tinkles clarity, the
truest music birds know:

I never want to throw out
the brook because it is
nearly dry or too noisy
so long as it
tells the truth, an
accuracy of all the other
dispositions, hills, marshes,
declivities, undergound ways
of the terrain surround, an
instantaneous, just summary
and announcement:

art is not nature
but the flow, brook-like, in the mind
is nature
and should it be
superhumanly swollen

to art's grandeurs when the accuracies
(absolute) of nature please
suitably to our context: an
ear of corn too high or heavy
is not worth planting:
art too strong or weak
betrays the living man:

poetry that wrestles
down all but a few
has its holding: but
the people, where they
turn their attention,
that is humanity:

our chief light
will put out
its light by
first putting too
much light out

I should be buying something
I go on paying

spells narrow in   if all is appearance
on sayings and   it is still without
catch the feeling   liberty for we must
say the exact air
of this & that mere
illusion

gardeners aren't fairweatherers
for weeds work
the cold, damp, cloudy days

like weeds as
much as roses
and you never
lack for liking

Considering the Variety

Considering the variety,
nicety, formal hardness,
careful contours of things
(how sight is filled with
the apparency of these) one
wonders about the byways of flow,
not much yelling of change
noticeable, dead trees (live
housing—will vines start
to dead trees) standing
hard, sun- and wind-rinsed:
the rumor of flow, one
wonders if invisibility
supresses that, wind, water
carrying on, rearranging,
both clear, sometimes muddy,
dusty, leaf-shown: and
underground, a stirring,
melting:
    is flux invisible to be
    kept out of sight
    or to emphasize the made:
    would designed
finery lose its strut and hard
joyousness if it
lost majority: still, not an item,
not even the stones, has not been often
milled away and away, if come
back in a stone or divided
participating in many stones:
(the time at the heart of
stones is no greater, but purer,
than that of the wearing surface)
but whatever flow dissolves

flow also brought the
nourishment of, the great
spirits flow through our forms,
declaring themselves through us,
the freedom of sequence, the leap
from one to another, the
essential preserved:
   but considerable lamentation,
though most scenes are quiet,
lamentation of the inexplicable,
lamentation against recalcitrant
fact, that though nothing is lost,
nothing, still the particular
is, that self or shape, so
carefully contrived,
crumbled, collapsed, its flow
lost in flow:
in this contemplation not a
wall, board, or splinter
yields: the alternatives,
side to side, are blank:
here, with breakdown,
gaiety, contrivance, and
immortality are sustained:
earth turns the bitter, sour,
known
to the bright sweets
born of the dead:
for us, it is a life, a
death, okay, take or leave it:
we
hang steadfastly on:

        fresh out

kingdoms of light answer
to the fact

Variable Cloudiness Windy

Variable cloudiness windy
and cooler this afternoon
with showers occasionally
mixed with snow flurries

when I was young the silk
of my mind
hard as a peony head
unfurled
and wind bloomed the parachute:

the air-head tugged me
up,
tore my roots loose and drove
high, so high

I want to touch down now
and taste the ground
I want to take in
my silk
and ask where I am
before it is too late to know

big aurora last night, a beam
of light, then an aurora, with
a crown!
the end of the world!
every day
in a million eyes

Unisex

These days there's
only one sex and
I am neither one

a blue cloud went over and ice
poured down like hail for a minute

this combo day mixed January
and May, sleet and tulips

On Walks I Go a Long Way along

On walks I go a long way along
a side-shallow, hardly a ditch,
dandelions grow right down
with grass (separating out the
stones) into the pebbly bottom
and I think if I
were struck down there
it would not be so bad,
perhaps; some weed stubs might
dig into my cheek but I understand
that: the stones might rustle
a little, dry, if I stirred: and
grass might half-tickle my nose
but I am familiar with grass:
I would not like being
held down long but
after death finished, the grip
would slacken, birds would
fly over indifferent as a corpse,
a worm would find a bit
to stir here and there,
the sinews would loosen and
bone spill from bone:
I am familiar with dandelions
between my fingers, slugs
cool in the sockets' dark domes:

today was so beautiful, hazy
blue, cold, cold nectar in
the blossoms, the leaves limp
cold: fellow said to me this
morning a man has been known

to mow his lawn and shovel snow
here the same day in May

penetrate and get the
ball down low

One Trains Hard for

One trains hard for
inadvertency

the terrain falls away:
love like a flowering quince
or crabapple bush nowhere
erupts: local green
mixes with stone becoming
on the periphery
casket gray: though this is true
(I care nothing
but to tell what is true)
I am astonished
with gladness
to find the brook clear,
the ripples dark-backed,
scriptures of light
working the slate
floor,
flat scales opaque with revelation:
a grackle stands in the water
and drinks from between his feet:
I can hardly
forget the sound of the
nameplate that squeaks and clangs
on Mrs. Day's mailbox there
when the wind blows:
I bend over clasping my
knees and the old fellow,
friend, frizzled schnauzer
runs out of the driveway
and whines grievous
pleasure
stretching up toward my face:

he knows me: we were
friends last fall:
I am myself:
I am so scared and sad I can
hardly bear to speak
and yet delight breaks
falls through me
and drives me off laughing
down a dozen brooks:
nothing, not anything, will
get over into the high land
and while some may die
as if community-ward
none, not one, will miss
unpeopled oblivion:
(except that in not imagining
oblivion one
cannot enter it)
what a dancer the stem of the
whirling down will be!
I am free:
I feel free, I think:
my chains have healed into me
as wires heal into trees

the saving world
saves by moving,
lost, out of
the real world
which loses all

Will Firinger Be Kissed: Will

Will Firinger be kissed: will
Cézanne's house be itself or
melt into the mountains: will
art have liberty from government
help: how will things
proceed: how will other things
proceed: (provide, provide):
modern industrial debris!
acid thunderheads! nitric, sulphuric
rain! salamander
eggs burnt out in farm ponds: Whitman,
the midwestern flues, effluents,
Carl, spill crud into the processes,
the lakes, ponds, and ditches of the
northeast and who knows what
the northeast does: Walt,
the greatest country
isn't wide enough to
dilute greed or bridge it:
put a drop of
water in baby's soreeyes,
acid will scour th'infection out:
this billowing age enlightened
with smoke, our eyes open(ed) at last
to airy cinders: if
salamanders die,
flies will stifle corporate suites:

what do those little
critters with dust-fine
wings do on a drizzly damp day
like this
(hold their noses)   home ice

the dance is the narrative of
figuremotions the dancer
inscribes on the memory

the dancer is the dancer (stylus, pen)

that is one way how
the other way is never
I'm tired of loving alone

roots go to water
leaves to light
pulling the trunk hard
between them

mist-drizzly cold
the clouds brush hillbrush:
the horizon slips
through

If Walking through Birdy Trees

If walking through birdy trees
you stop, several still birds will burst
into flight, your motion, conserved,
communicated into lesser, faster speeds:
the more familiar
hemisphere, that if having been still you
move and birds or other animals
startle and fly, why I have
not decided what to make
of that: make something of it:
think it over and out:
hold the same thread through numerous terrains,
transfigurations, etc.
and see to how many
oceanic possibilities a strand
applies:
not to hold onto the strand you have is to seem
dismissive, cutting, as if you
liked not all of reality's
clothes but only
certain patches or
threads, whole colth, a
cheapening: no matter what
intelligence went into making
the maze if
the one thread leads you out

They Say It Snowed

They say it snowed
a few days ago
a bit, one of
those rainy cold
days when skinny droplets
flurred into feathery
fluff,
whitening streaks
out of the dismal
downward descending

the lords of volition slice
down Hanshaw
in the after midnight (close
to dawn, now) hours,
toss beer cans, cigarette
packs, liquor bottles into
the ditch without a thought
for any nature than their
own: and specially into the
bushy border by the brook
the alarming discards of
passion fly: the early
day, when passion is spent,
pent, or bent
shows the brook circling
silver canfish:

the lords of volition care for
the brooks that burst their
breasts, the churning and flowing
there, the spills and stalls,
urgencies not of matter, wind
ripplings

I pick up after them and find
the slug has made a home under
the gumwrapper or grass is
holding and hiding a
Schaefer can
filled with the plump, pulp
bellies of mosquito larvae:
    the lords of volition
    caring for their own
    natures care for nature
    around them; they expend,
satisfy, create: I pick
up, tearing their doings out
of time and context, for a
neat ditch with clipped banks

lunch reservoirs on our rears

overlook   to set our feet
look over   on symbolic rock,
              solid space—
              that is the heave

I am so backward   how many
in my correspondence should I
I have to stand in line   put you
to hear from myself   down for

we (l) come